Hot Air, Don't Care!

AMAZING AIR FRYER MEALS IN MINUTES

CENTENNIAL KITCHEN®

CENTENNIAL BOOKS

SEE P.51

Loaded Potato Skins
With Avocado

Hot Air, Don't Care!

AMAZING AIR FRYER MEALS IN MINUTES

SEE P.101

Southern-Style
Catfish With Caper
Tartar Sauce

CONTENTS

16

48

62

80

123

128

Cooking With AIR

FROM HEARTY MAIN MEALS TO DELICIOUS DESSERTS, THERE'S NO SHORTAGE OF WHAT YOU CAN COOK UP IN AN AIR FRYER—AND IN JUST 30 MINUTES OR LESS!

Air fryers have become huge sellers both online and in stores since 2010, when the Philips electronic company distributed the first model. And every year, more home cooks are delighted to discover all the ways this simple appliance can make nearly all the foods they love with little to no added fat—and in much less time, to boot.

Whether you're a longtime fan or you're thinking about investigating just how much magic there could possibly be in this handy gadget, it's always the right time to check out new recipes. Although the air fryer's early fame came from its ability to make nearly greaseless fried foods, it's got a whole world of superpowers, from cooking up a juicy steak to baking a delicious blueberry pie. And with more features being added to products all the time, there's no limit to what you can serve up in your own kitchen.

An air fryer is like a small convection oven. It cooks food by circulating hot air. And in this book, you'll find recipes for mouthwatering dishes from breakfast (such as French Toast With Raspberries,

Maple Syrup and Butter, page 16) to dessert (Glazed Doughnuts, page 137). Plus, discover plenty of creative appetizers (Cheesy Tomato Bruschetta, page 30, and Fried Pickle Chips, page 38) and entrées (Pork Schnitzel, page 71; General Tso's Chicken, page 79; or Crabcakes, page 96). And don't forget the sides, such as Mexican Street Corn (page 114) or Garlic Parmesan Asparagus (page 124). Got a snack attack? Satisfy your cravings from salty (Soft Pretzels, page 45) to sweet (Cinnamon Sugar Apple Chips, page 51).

Best of all, each recipe in this book takes no more than 30 minutes to make, so you can have a delicious meal on the table in a flash, whether it's for yourself, your whole family or a party that you're hosting. It takes just one simple appliance to do all of your cooking for the day—not to mention how easy the air fryer is to clean!

These recipes were created for a 5.25-quart air fryer with a 60-minute timer; consult your owner's manual to adjust recipes as needed. We know you'll enjoy making—and devouring!—these yummy dishes as much as we did. Enjoy!

THE CONVECTION HEAT FROM AN AIR FRYER COOKS FOOD FASTER AND CREATES A GORGEOUS CRISP COATING WHEN DESIRED.

SEE P.137

Caramelized Bananas With Ice Cream

Learning the
BASICS

<u>READY TO GET UP AND RUNNING WITH YOUR NEW AIR FRYER? HERE ARE A FEW TIPS TO GET YOU STARTED. CHECK YOUR USER MANUAL FOR ADDITIONAL DETAILS ON SAFETY AND SETUP, AS WELL AS FOR GENERAL CARE AND CLEANING TIPS.</u>

SOME AIR FRYER MODELS WORK LIKE A TOASTER AND CAN ALSO BE USED TO BAKE, BROIL AND (YES) MAKE TOAST.

OVERVIEW

An air fryer is versatile and multifunctional. It works like a convection oven, so you can use it on many dishes that are usually prepared in a regular oven. But before you begin, read through the owner's manual and familiarize yourself with the temperature and timer settings on your fryer. (Your model may have more bells and whistles for you to explore later.)

Since your fryer might be a different size than the one we used, recipes might need more or less cooking time. So when the timer goes off, carefully remove the basket of food from the fryer and place it on a level, heatproof surface. If it's not cooked to your liking, return the basket to the fryer and reset the timer dial for additional cooking time.

If a recipe calls for shaking the basket during cooking, remove the basket from the fryer and gently jiggle it from side to side, then replace it in the fryer.

WORKING

TIMER

5 · 25
0 · 30

MOST AIR FRYER
MODELS OFFER A
TIMER AND A VARIETY
OF TEMPERATURE
SETTINGS FOR
DIFFERENT FOODS.

250° | 325°

175° 400°F

TEMP

OFF

Cook's Notes

Today's air fryers are more
versatile than ever: Top-of-the-line
models do everything but
the dishes. **On a budget?**
Quite a few brands have introduced
lower-priced machines.

SEE P.118

Creamy Mac
and Cheese

French Fries

SEE P.123

Cook's Notes

Sure, an air fryer makes **awesome french fries**. But this gadget does so much more. Remember, it's a small convection oven—so it can make everything from a cake to a roast to **perfect mac and cheese**!

NOTE Oil and juices may collect in the basket holder during cooking; this is to be expected and does not affect the cooking process.

TIPS & TRICKS

★ Fryer components may be hot to the touch, so always use oven mitts! Use heat-resistant kitchen tongs to remove fragile or large ingredients from the basket after cooking.
★ If you need to check the food while it's cooking, or when you think it's done, always remove the basket carefully; it will be hot!
★ To help prevent foods from sticking to the basket, lightly coat the basket with cooking spray before cooking. (Consider purchasing a mister to fill with your favorite oil.)

AIR FRYERS ARE MULTITASKERS!

Air fryer makers have taken a cue from Instant Pot's success by adding even more functions. Some brands offer an air fryer/toaster oven combo that can hold a 9x13-inch pan; others do double duty as an air fryer and a pressure cooker; and some even have multiple zones, so your french fries can cook in the lower pan while your chicken gets nicely roasted up top.

SEE
P.14

Baked Egg Cups

YUMMY
BREAKFASTS

RISE AND SHINE WITH ONE OF THESE TASTY MEAL IDEAS—SWEET OR SAVORY—ALL MADE EASY WITH THE HELP OF YOUR AIR FRYER.

BAKED EGG CUPS

EASY | FAST FIX

These cups, filled with hearty, thick-cut bacon and eggs, help you serve up a hot meal in a hurry.

Start to finish 15 minutes (3 active)
Servings 6

	Cooking spray
6	thick-cut bacon slices
6	eggs
	Salt and freshly ground black pepper, to taste
1	small bunch chives, halved
2	tablespoons cress, snipped

1 Preheat air fryer to 330 F. Arrange six silicone heating cups (or paper cupcake liners) in basket; spray with cooking spray.
2 Line with a bacon slice before carefully cracking an egg into each cup. Season with salt and pepper.
3 Cook for 10–12 minutes until eggs are set.
4 Carefully remove baked cups from air fryer and garnish with chives and cress before serving.

CREAMY SCRAMBLED EGGS

EASY | FAST FIX

Upgrade your scrambled eggs by adding heavy cream! It doesn't take much of the cream to add amazing richness to this simple dish.

Start to finish 17 minutes
(5 minutes active)
Servings 4

2	tablespoons unsalted butter
8	large eggs
4	tablespoons heavy cream
	Salt
	Freshly ground black pepper
	Toast, for serving

1 Preheat air fryer to 220 F.
2 Working in two batches, place 1 tablespoon butter in a 6-inch cake pan. Melt in air fryer, about 1 minute.
3 Remove pan from air fryer and add four eggs, 2 tablespoons cream, and plenty of salt and pepper, beating with a fork.
4 Return pan to air fryer and cook for 2 minutes. Remove pan, scramble with a fork until partially set, and return to air fryer for an additional 2–3 minutes until eggs are scrambled to your liking.
5 Repeat steps 2–4 for remaining scrambled eggs. Serve immediately with warm toast on the side.

BUTTERMILK BISCUITS

CROWD-PLEASER | FAMILY FAVORITE

Nothing says good morning like buttery biscuits—they're soft, satisfying and perfect! These golden goodies will add a homey, old-fashioned touch to your table.

Start to finish 25 minutes
(15 minutes active)
Servings 6

1¼	cups all-purpose flour, plus extra for dusting
½	cup cake flour
½	teaspoon baking powder
¼	teaspoon baking soda
1	teaspoon white sugar
½	teaspoon salt
¼	cup unsalted butter, cold and cubed, plus 1 tablespoon melted
¾	cup buttermilk
	Cooking spray
	Jam or jelly, for serving

1 Over a large mixing bowl, sift flours, baking powder, baking soda, sugar and salt. Stir to combine.
2 Add butter cubes and rub into the flour mixture until pea-sized pieces of butter and flour form. Gently stir in buttermilk with a spatula until a rough dough forms.
3 Sprinkle flour over a work surface. Place dough on top and sprinkle with more flour before flattening into a ½-inch-thick round.
4 Cut out 2½-inch circles with a large cookie cutter (approximately 6 circles total). Place parchment in the air fryer basket and coat with cooking spray.
5 Arrange biscuit circles on parchment and brush with melted butter. Preheat air fryer to 400 F.
6 Cook biscuits until golden brown, about 8–10 minutes, gently shaking basket halfway through cooking.
7 Remove when ready and let cool briefly before serving warm with jam or jelly.

VEGETARIAN FRITTATA

CROWD-PLEASER | EASY | FAST FIX

Don't feel limited by the vegetables listed here! Experiment to find ones you like. If you're making several of these savory dishes for a crowd, try adding different veggies to each.

Start to finish 25 minutes
(5 minutes active)
Servings 4

	Cooking spray
4	large eggs
7	tablespoons milk
	Salt
	Freshly ground black pepper
8	cherry tomatoes
1	cup baby spinach, washed
½	cup shredded cheese, such as Monterey Jack

1 Preheat air fryer to 350 F. Coat a 6-inch baking pan with cooking spray.
2 Add eggs, milk and plenty of salt and pepper to taste to baking pan and beat well. Arrange cherry tomatoes and spinach in egg mixture and sprinkle cheese on top.
3 Cook frittata for 17–20 minutes, checking after 12 minutes, until eggs are set and frittata is golden at the edges.
4 Remove pan from air fryer and carefully turn out frittata onto a plate. Cool slightly and cut into 4 portions before serving.

THESE BISCUITS ARE A
WELCOME ADDITION TO
YOUR BREAKFAST—
ESPECIALLY WITH SOME
TANGY MARMALADE!

Buttermilk
Biscuits

FRENCH TOAST WITH RASPBERRIES, MAPLE SYRUP AND BUTTER

CROWD-PLEASER | EASY | FAMILY FAVORITE

You can leave your griddle in the kitchen cabinet! An air fryer will cook your French toast to perfection—and with its garnish of fresh fruit, you'll feel like you're having breakfast and dessert at the same time!

Start to finish 30 minutes
(10 minutes active)
Servings 4

4	**eggs**
⅔	**cup milk**
2	**teaspoons vanilla extract**
1	**teaspoon ground cinnamon**
1	**pinch ground nutmeg**
8	**white bread slices, stale, cut into triangles**
	Butter, maple syrup and fresh raspberries, for serving

1 Preheat air fryer to 360 F. Line basket with a sheet of parchment.
2 In a shallow bowl, beat together eggs, milk, vanilla and spices until mixture is well combined.
3 Working in two batches, dip four bread triangles in beaten eggs, turning to coat. Let excess drip off before arranging in basket in a single layer.
4 Cook for 5 minutes, shaking basket a few times during cooking. Turn and cook for another 5 minutes until golden brown. Repeat steps 3 and 4 for the second batch.
5 When ready to serve, stack on plates, top with butter, and serve with maple syrup and fresh raspberries.

QUICK TIP

Use stale bread slices! They won't turn soggy when dipped into beaten egg mixture.

Cook's Notes

Why not branch out from white bread for your French toast? A thick-cut **brioche or challah** loaf adds texture and a little sweetness. Or try a **baguette**; cut it on the diagonal for larger slices.

Breakfast Potatoes

Giant Breakfast Burrito

CREAM CHEESE FROSTING AND COLORFUL SPRINKLES TURN THE MORNING INTO A PARTY!

STRAWBERRY TARTS

FAMILY FAVORITE | KID-FRIENDLY

These are so much tastier than the store-bought versions! Just make sure these tarts have cooled before you remove them from the air fryer. If not, they may break.

Start to finish 25 minutes
(15 minutes active)
Servings 3

- 1   (14.1-ounce) package refrigerated pie crust (2 crusts)
- ⅓   cup strawberry preserves
- 2   teaspoons cornstarch
    Cooking spray
- ½   cup sour cream
- 1   ounce cream cheese, softened
- 1   teaspoon sugar
- 1   teaspoon sprinkles

1 Lay both pie crusts on a working surface. Using a pizza cutter, cut into 3 rectangles per crust (6 total rectangles).
2 In a small bowl, stir together preserves and cornstarch.
3 Place 1 tablespoon of preserve mixture in the upper area of 3 crusts.
4 Top with remaining 3 crusts to form tarts.
5 Crimp all edges with a fork.
6 Place tarts in air fryer, spray with cooking spray and cook at 375 F for 8–10 minutes.
7 Meanwhile, combine sour cream, cream cheese and sugar until smooth.
8 Allow tarts to cool in air fryer.
9 Remove from air fryer to cooling rack. Spread frosting over tarts and top with sprinkles.

QUICK TIP

You can freeze these fruit tarts and then warm them up in a toaster oven when you want a fast breakfast on the go for the kids (or yourself!).

Mini Blueberry Muffins

HOSTING A BRUNCH? THESE TINY MUFFINS LET EVERYONE HAVE A TASTE WITHOUT FILLING UP BEFORE THE MAIN DISH.

Start to finish 10 minutes
(1 minute active)
Servings 12

- 1 **(12-ounce) package sausage patties, uncooked**
  Cooking spray

1 Place sausage patties in air fryer basket or racks. Coat with cooking spray.
2 Cook at 400 F for 5 minutes. Turn sausage and cook another 3–4 minutes or until browned and thermometer reads 160 F. Remove from air fryer.

EASY CHEESE OMELET

CLASSIC | FAMILY FAVORITE

This omelet cooks up so fluffy in an air fryer! Feel free to substitute your favorite cheeses, such as Monterey Jack or crumbled goat cheese; you can also add in extra veggies.

Start to finish 20 minutes
(10 minutes active)
Servings 1

- 3 **eggs**
- ¼ **cup milk**
- ¼ **teaspoon salt**
- ¼ **teaspoon ground black pepper**
- 1 **tablespoon minced scallions**
- ⅓ **cup shredded cheddar cheese**
- ⅓ **cup shredded mozzarella cheese**
  GARNISHES Bacon slices, crumbled Sausage Patties (see recipe below left), sliced scallions, chopped tomato

1 In a small bowl, mix the eggs, milk, salt and pepper until combined.
2 Stir in scallions and cheeses.
3 Pour into a 6-inch well-greased cake pan.
4 Place pan in air fryer basket or rack and cook at 350 F for 8–10 minutes.
5 Use a spatula to loosen omelet from the sides of pan and transfer to a plate. Fold omelet over.
6 Garnish with bacon, sausage, sliced scallions and tomato, if desired.

MINI BLUEBERRY MUFFINS

CLASSIC | PARTY FARE

A silicone mini-muffin pan helps these streusel-topped muffins cook evenly—and makes cleanup a breeze, too. For a sweeter variety, add in a quarter cup of mini chocolate chips.

Start to finish 25 minutes
(10 minutes active)
Servings 12 muffins

- 1 **cup flour**
- 1 **teaspoon baking powder**
- 2 **tablespoons sugar**
- 2 **eggs**
- 2 **teaspoons vanilla extract**
- ⅓ **cup milk**
- 3 **tablespoons melted butter**
- ¾ **cup blueberries**
  Cooking spray
- 1 **tablespoon brown sugar**
- 1 **tablespoon sugar**
- 1 **tablespoon flour**
- 1 **tablespoon cold butter, cut into small pieces**

1 Preheat air fryer to 320 F.
2 Mix flour and next 7 ingredients in a mixing bowl until well combined.
3 Coat a 12-cup silicone mini-muffin pan with cooking spray. Pour batter into prepared pan, filling each cup two-thirds of the way full.
4 In another bowl, combine sugars, flour and butter until crumbly.
5 Sprinkle on top of muffins.
6 Place in air fryer basket or racks and cook for 12–14 minutes or until wooden pick comes out clean.
7 Remove muffins from air fryer and serve warm.

SAUSAGE PATTIES

COMFORT FOOD | EASY

There's no splatter or mess when you brown sausage in an air fryer!

Cook's Notes

The cheese you choose to use in an omelet is entirely up to you; however, bear in mind that **some cheeses melt better than others.** For the creamiest omelets, opt for cheddar, mozzarella, Brie, fontina or Gruyère.

Easy Cheese Omelet

Cook's Notes

If you enjoy baking muffins and cupcakes, consider getting a set of **silicone baking cups**. They're reusable—no paper waste!—and come in assorted sizes. Some should be used in a tin, but others can be used freestanding.

Lemon Poppy Seed Mini Muffins

LEMON POPPY SEED MINI MUFFINS

CLASSIC | EASY | PARTY FARE

These mini muffins are refreshingly tangy.

Start to finish 17 minutes
(5 minutes active)
Servings 12

- ⅓ cup sugar
- 1 tablespoon lemon zest
- 1 tablespoon lemon juice
- 1 cup all-purpose flour
- 1 teaspoon baking powder
- ¼ teaspoon baking soda
- ½ teaspoon salt
- ⅓ cup sour cream
- 1 egg
- 1 teaspoon vanilla extract
- ⅓ cup butter, melted
- 1 tablespoon poppy seeds

1 Preheat air fryer to 320 F.
2 In a small bowl, mix sugar, lemon zest and juice, flour, baking powder, baking soda and salt until blended.
3 In a medium bowl, mix together sour cream, egg, vanilla and butter until blended. Fold dry mixture into wet; mix well. Stir in poppy seeds.
4 Line mini muffin tin with paper liners. Fill each liner about three-quarters full with batter. Place tin in air fryer.
5 Cook for 12 minutes, or until a toothpick inserted in center of muffin comes out clean.
6 Let cool before serving.

BAKED EGGS IN BELL PEPPERS

EASY | FAMILY FAVORITE | HEALTHY

How clever! Eggs served in a bell pepper boat make for a cute presentation—and an extra serving of veggies, to boot!

Start to finish 20 minutes
(5 minutes active)
Servings 2

Cooking spray
- 1 bell pepper, halved and seeded
- 4 eggs
- ¼ teaspoon salt
- ¼ teaspoon ground black pepper
- ¼ cup shredded cheddar cheese

1 Coat bell pepper halves with cooking spray.
2 Crack two eggs into each bell pepper half.
3 Sprinkle with salt and pepper.
4 Place bell pepper in air fryer basket or racks and cook at 325 F for 15 minutes.
5 Remove from air fryer and top with shredded cheese.

SPINACH AND TOMATO FRITTATA

CLASSIC | EASY

Getting your first serving of leafy greens at breakfast makes a healthy start to the day. This frittata is also a good option for a light lunch.

Start to finish 25 minutes
(10 minutes active)
Servings 2

- 4 large eggs
- ¼ cup half-and-half
- ½ teaspoon kosher salt
- ¼ teaspoon ground black pepper
- 2 cups baby spinach
- ½ cup diced white onion
- ¼ cup diced tomato
- ½ cup shredded cheddar cheese
  Cooking spray
  Sliced scallions, optional

1 Preheat air fryer to 360 F.
2 In a medium bowl, whisk together eggs, half-and-half, salt and pepper; stir in spinach, onion, tomato and cheese and mix well.
3 Coat a nonstick 6-inch round pan with cooking spray. Pour egg mixture into pan.
4 Cook eggs in air fryer until frittata is set, 15–18 minutes.
5 Top frittata with scallions before serving, if desired.

CINNAMON ROLLS

EASY | FAMILY FAVORITE

Shhh! These delightful treats are made with a tube of refrigerated crescent rolls—especially with that cream cheese glaze on top!

Start to finish 30 minutes
(20 minutes active)
Servings 6

- 2 tablespoons butter, melted
- ⅓ cup packed brown sugar
- ½ teaspoon cinnamon
- ⅛ teaspoon salt
- 1 (8-ounce) tube refrigerated crescent rolls
  Cooking spray
- 3 ounces cream cheese, softened
- ½ cup powdered sugar
- 2 tablespoons half-and-half

1 Combine butter, brown sugar, cinnamon and salt.
2 On a lightly floured surface, roll out crescent dough in one piece. Pinch seams together and fold in half. Roll dough into a 9x7-inch rectangle.
3 Spread butter mixture over dough, leaving ¼-inch border.
4 From long side, roll dough like a jelly roll, then cut crosswise into 6 pieces.
5 Arrange rolls in air fryer basket or rack sprayed with cooking spray.
6 Cook at 350 F for 10 minutes or until golden. Remove to a wire rack.
7 Meanwhile, in a small bowl combine cream cheese, powdered sugar and half-and-half until smooth.
8 Spread glaze over warm cinnamon rolls and serve.

QUICK TIP

You can use light or dark brown sugar in most recipes—the darker kind has more molasses and a more complex flavor.

AMAZING
APPETIZERS & SNACKS

WHETHER YOU'RE HOSTING A PARTY OR JUST LOOKING FOR A QUICK TREAT, THESE SMALL BITES COME TOGETHER IN A SNAP.

SEE P.30

Supreme Tater Tots

Barbecue
Potato Chips

a mixing bowl. Add tomatoes and some salt and pepper to taste, stirring thoroughly to combine.

3 Top baguette slices with shredded mozzarella. Arrange half of the bruschetta slices on wire rack.

4 Cook for 5–7 minutes until cheese is golden brown. Remove from air fryer and top with dressed tomato mixture.

5 Repeat step 4 for remaining bruschetta. When ready to serve, garnish with a sprinkle of dried oregano.

BARBECUE POTATO CHIPS

CROWD-PLEASER | KID-FRIENDLY

Russets are your best choice for potato chips; their long, oval shape means you'll get consistently sized slices that cook evenly. Using a mandoline to slice the potatoes will ensure thin and crispy chips.

Start to finish 30 minutes
(15 minutes active)
Servings 4

1 large russet potato, peeled and thinly sliced
1 tablespoon barbecue seasoning
½ teaspoon salt
 Cooking spray

1 Sprinkle potato slices generously with barbecue seasoning and salt.

2 Place in air fryer basket or racks (you may need to work in batches).

3 Coat with cooking spray; cook at 400 F for 15 minutes or until golden brown and crisp, flipping halfway through cooking. Remove from fryer.

QUICK TIP

Look for barbecue seasoning in the spice section of your supermarket; several brands make versions of this blend. Try it on fries and onion rings, too.

SUPREME TATER TOTS

EASY | KID-FRIENDLY

If you're tired of dipping your tater tots in ketchup, give them this melty, cheesy upgrade.

Start to finish 15 minutes
(5 minutes active)
Servings 4

 Cooking spray
2 cups frozen tater tots
 GARNISHES Cheddar cheese, cooked bacon crumbles, sour cream, sliced scallions, snipped chives

1 Lightly spray air fryer basket with cooking spray. Place tots in basket in a single layer (you may need to work in batches).

2 Cook at 350 F for 10 minutes, shaking the basket or rack halfway through.

3 Remove tater tots from air fryer and place on a platter.

4 Top with cheddar cheese, bacon, sour cream, scallions and chives to serve.

CHEESY TOMATO BRUSCHETTA

CROWD-PLEASER | FAST FIX

These toasted bread slices, topped with fresh tomatoes and cheese, are always a party favorite.

Start to finish 25 minutes
(10 minutes active)
Servings 4

3 tablespoons extra-virgin olive oil
1 large garlic clove, minced
3 large tomatoes, cored, seeded and diced
 Salt and freshly ground black pepper, to taste
1 large baguette, cut on bias into eight slices
1 cup shredded mozzarella
 Dried oregano

1 Preheat air fryer to 360 F. Line basket with parchment paper and set a wire rack or trivet in it.

2 Stir together olive oil and garlic in

Cheesy
Tomato
Bruschetta

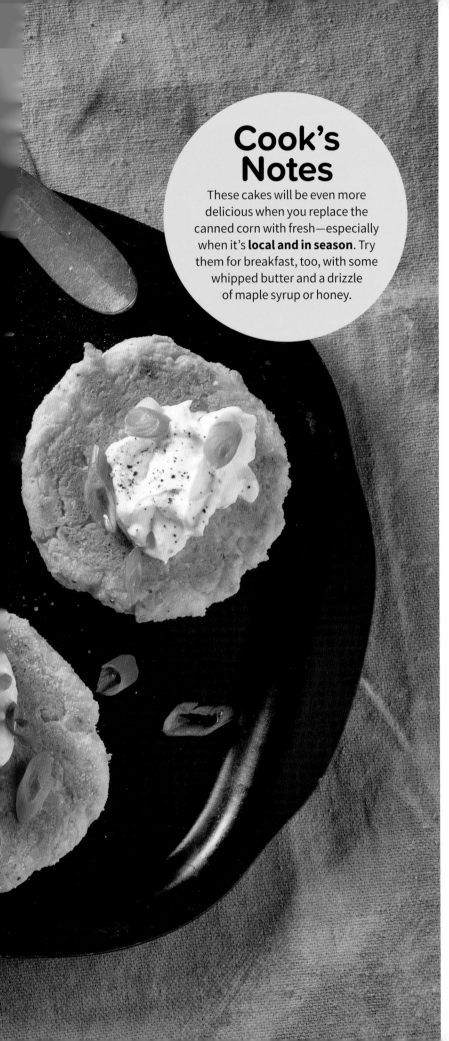

Cook's Notes

These cakes will be even more delicious when you replace the canned corn with fresh—especially when it's **local and in season**. Try them for breakfast, too, with some whipped butter and a drizzle of maple syrup or honey.

CORN FRITTER CAKES

COMFORT FOOD | EASY | KID-FRIENDLY

These savory cakes have irresistibly crisp edges.

Start to finish 30 minutes
(30 minutes active)
Servings 10

- 2   eggs
- 1   teaspoon sugar
- 1   teaspoon salt
- ½   teaspoon ground black pepper
- ½   cup all-purpose flour
- 1   teaspoon baking powder
- 1   (16-ounce) can whole-kernel corn, drained and rinsed
- 1   cup shredded cheddar cheese
- 3   tablespoons butter, melted
- 1   jalapeño, diced
     Cooking spray
     GARNISHES Sour cream, cracked black pepper, chopped scallions, optional

1 In a medium bowl, mix together eggs, sugar, salt, pepper, flour and baking powder.
2 Stir in corn, cheese, butter and jalapeño. Shape into 10 patties. If time allows, place in freezer for 30 minutes.
3 Meanwhile, preheat air fryer to 400 F. Coat basket or tray with cooking spray.
4 Place patties in basket (you may need to work in batches). Cook for 10 minutes; flip and cook an additional 5 minutes.
5 Serve with sour cream, black pepper and scallions, if desired.

⌄⌄

QUICK TIP

Spice up these fritters with some of your favorite flavors, such as Cajun seasoning, cayenne pepper, garlic or onion powder, and even ground cinnamon and sugar.

FRIED RAVIOLI

FAMILY FAVORITE | FAST FIX

Turn ravioli into finger food! Frying makes the pasta crispy, and the cheese melted and yummy.

Start to finish 25 minutes
(10 minutes active)
Servings 4

- 1   cup all-purpose flour
- 1   teaspoon Italian seasoning
     Salt, to taste
- 2   eggs
- 2   cups seasoned breadcrumbs
- 16 frozen cheese ravioli
     Cooking spray
     Marinara sauce, for dipping

1 Preheat air fryer to 360 F.
2 Place flour in a shallow dish and stir in Italian seasoning and some salt to taste. Beat eggs with some salt in a second shallow dish. Place seasoned breadcrumbs in a third shallow dish.
3 Dust frozen ravioli in seasoned flour, shaking off excess. Dip into beaten egg, let excess drip off, and then dredge in breadcrumbs to coat.
4 Coat ravioli on both sides with cooking spray before arranging in air fryer basket (you may need to work in batches).
5 Cook for 15 minutes, turning after 8 minutes, until golden brown and cooked through.
6 Remove from air fryer and let cool briefly on a cooling rack before serving with cups of warm marinara sauce.

JALAPEÑO POPPERS

EASY | PARTY FARE

The peppers can be stuffed ahead of time and stored in the fridge until you're ready to air-fry them— which will come in handy if you're making enough for a crowd!

Start to finish 25 minutes
(15 minutes active)
Servings 4

- 2   ounces cream cheese, softened
- ¼   cup finely chopped cooked chicken
- ¼   cup shredded cheddar cheese
- ¼   cup minced scallions
- 1   tablespoon hot sauce
- 4   large jalapeños, halved lengthwise and seeds scraped
- 2   tablespoons panko breadcrumbs

1 In a bowl, stir together cream cheese, chicken, cheddar, scallions and hot sauce until well combined.
2 Stuff jalapeños with cream cheese mixture. Sprinkle with breadcrumbs.
3 Coat air fryer basket or racks with cooking spray.
4 Cook at 370 F until tops are browned and peppers are tender, about 10 minutes.

ONION RINGS

EASY | KID-FRIENDLY

The buttermilk brings out the sweetness of the onions.

Start to finish 25 minutes
(10 minutes active)
Servings 2

- ½   cup flour
- 1   teaspoon salt
- ½   teaspoon pepper
- ½   cup buttermilk
- 1   egg
- 1   cup panko breadcrumbs
- 2   tablespoons vegetable oil
- 1   large sweet onion, cut into ½-inch-thick slices and separated into rings
     Cooking spray

1 You'll need 3 shallow bowls: In the first, combine flour, salt and pepper; in the second, beat buttermilk and egg; in the third, mix breadcrumbs and oil.
2 Dredge onion rings in flour mixture, then in buttermilk mixture and then in breadcrumbs.
3 Place rings in single layer in air fryer basket (you may need to work in batches). Coat rings with cooking spray.
4 Cook at 400 F for 15 minutes. Flip halfway through.

Onion Rings

Cook's Notes

It's never a bad idea to have a half-dozen or so hard-boiled eggs in the fridge. They're packed with protein and other nutrients, so they're **an ideal snack**, but they're also ready to be made into egg salad or deviled eggs.

Hard-Boiled Eggs

HARD-BOILED EGGS

EASY | FAST FIX

No worries about the pot boiling over when you use the air fryer!

Start to finish 20 minutes
(1 minute active)
Servings 6

    6   large eggs

1 Place the eggs in air fryer basket or racks.
2 Cook at 250 F for 16 minutes. Remove and add to an ice bath.
3 Peel once cool enough to handle.

PIGS IN BLANKETS

FAMILY FAVORITE | FAST FIX

Serve these tasty treats with an assortment of dipping sauces on the side. Mustard is a classic choice, but horseradish aioli adds a real kick.

Start to finish 25 minutes
(15 minutes active)
Servings 4

    8   large cocktail franks
    1   (8-ounce) tube refrigerated
        crescent rolls
        All-purpose flour, for dusting
        Cooking spray

1 Thoroughly pat cocktail franks dry with paper towels.
2 Roll out crescent roll dough on a lightly floured surface into an 8x8-inch square. Cut out eight 1-inch-wide strips from the dough.
3 Coat cocktail franks with cooking spray before wrapping the dough strips around them.
4 Preheat air fryer to 330 F. Arrange wrapped franks in basket and coat with more cooking spray.
5 Cook for 10–12 minutes until dough is golden, turning halfway through.
6 Remove from air fryer when ready and let cool briefly before serving.

Pigs in Blankets

GARLIC BREAD

CROWD-PLEASER | FAMILY FAVORITE

The scent of garlic bread will bring everyone to the dinner table! For a twist, sprinkle on some Parmesan.

Start to finish 15 minutes
(10 minutes active)
Servings 4

    ⅓   cup butter, softened
    2   small garlic cloves, minced
    1   handful fresh parsley, chopped
    ½   teaspoon salt
    4   dinner rolls, split

1 Preheat air fryer to 400 F.
2 Using a fork, mash together butter, garlic, parsley and salt in a small mixing bowl until thoroughly combined.
3 Spread mixture onto cut sides of dinner roll halves, reassembling rolls afterward.
4 Line air fryer basket with parchment paper; place rolls in basket. Cook for 6–7 minutes until golden and crisp.
5 Remove from air fryer to cooling rack. Let cool briefly before serving.

STUFFED MUSHROOMS

CLASSIC | FAST FIX

Filled with a mix of three cheeses, these make a great appetizer or a party snack.

Start to finish 20 minutes
(10 minutes active)
Servings 4

- 1 (8-ounce) package whole fresh large mushrooms
- ½ (8-ounce) package cream cheese, softened
- ¼ cup grated Parmesan cheese
- ¼ cup cheddar cheese
- ¼ cup chopped, cooked bacon
- 1 teaspoon Worcestershire sauce
- 1 teaspoon minced garlic
  GARNISH Chopped parsley

1 Cut the stems out of the mushrooms. Gently clean with damp paper towels.
2 In a bowl, mix together remaining ingredients.
3 Stuff mushrooms with cheese mixture.
4 Place in air fryer basket or rack and cook at 375 F for 8 minutes.
5 Garnish with chopped parsley and serve hot.

CORN TORTILLA CHIPS

CROWD-PLEASER | FAMILY FAVORITE

Nothing beats fresh tortilla chips— and with an air fryer, you get the crunchy goodness without much fat.

Start to finish 15 minutes
(10 minutes active)
Servings 4

- 4 (6-inch) corn tortillas
- 2 tablespoons canola oil
  Sea salt, to taste

1 Preheat air fryer to 400 F.
2 Cut tortillas into triangles with a sharp knife. Brush with oil and season with a sprinkle of salt.
3 Arrange half of the tortilla triangles in basket. Cook for 3–4 minutes until crisp, shaking basket a few times during cooking.
4 When cooked, spread out on a cooling rack. Repeat cooking for remaining tortilla chips.
5 Serve warm or at room temperature with salsa or guacamole.

POTATO LATKES

FAMILY FAVORITE | KID-FRIENDLY

These crispy and savory "potato pancakes" are a traditional Jewish food. Serve them with sour cream, or try topping with applesauce.

Start to finish 30 minutes
(15 minutes active)
Servings 4

- 3 large russet potatoes, peeled
- 2 eggs
- 1 teaspoon kosher salt, divided
- 3 tablespoons matzo meal
- 1 tablespoon potato starch, plus extra for dusting
  Cooking spray
  Sour cream or applesauce, for serving
- 1 tablespoon chives, snipped

1 Coarsely grate potatoes on a box grater, or use grater attachment on a food processor for uniform pieces.
2 Submerge grated potatoes in a bowl of cold water. Drain well and wring out in a clean dish towel to extract as much moisture as possible.
3 In a large mixing bowl, beat eggs with ½ teaspoon salt. Whisk in matzo meal and potato starch.
4 Add grated potatoes to egg mixture, stirring thoroughly to combine. Divide and shape into 4 large latkes, approximately ¼-inch thick.
5 Dust with more potato starch, gently shaking or brushing off excess. Season with remaining salt.
6 Preheat air fryer to 380 F. Coat basket with cooking spray before carefully arranging latkes in it.
7 Cook for 8 minutes. Turn and cook for an additional 4–6 minutes until golden brown all over.
8 Remove from air fryer and let cool briefly before serving with sour cream and chives or applesauce.

FRIED PICKLE CHIPS

CROWD-PLEASER | FAST FIX

Snack on these zesty chips with a creamy ranch dip or a spicy aioli.

Start to finish 25 minutes
(10 minutes active)
Servings 4

- 2 cups dill pickle slices, drained
- 1 egg
- 1 cup breadcrumbs
- ¼ cup Parmesan cheese, grated
- 1 teaspoon garlic powder
- ½ teaspoon dried oregano
- ½ teaspoon salt

1 Preheat air fryer to 400 F. Coat basket with cooking spray.
2 Thoroughly dry pickle slices with paper towels.
3 In a shallow bowl, beat egg with 1 tablespoon water.
4 In another shallow bowl, stir together remaining ingredients.
5 Dip pickle slices into egg, let excess drip off, then dredge in breadcrumb mixture.
6 Arrange pickle slices in basket (you may need to work in batches) and cook for 10–12 minutes until golden brown, gently shaking basket a few times during cooking.
7 Serve hot from the air fryer with the dip of your choice.

QUICK TIP

The secret to frying pickles is to dry them well before coating them—otherwise the coating will fall off when you cook them.

Fried Pickle Chips

Cook's Notes

Looking for a dip to complement these **fried plantains**? Try a traditional **mojo sauce**. It's got an olive oil base and is loaded with garlic, herbs and citrus juices—delicious and easy to make (or purchase)!

PLANTAIN BITES

CROWD-PLEASER | FAST FIX

Plantains are usually served cooked, due to their high starch content.

Start to finish 25 minutes
(10 minutes active)
Servings 4

2	**large plantains**
	Cooking spray
2–3	**tablespoons coconut oil, melted**
2–3	**tablespoons brown sugar**
1–3	**teaspoons jerk seasoning**

1 Peel and cut the plantains into ¼-inch thick slices. Coat basket or rack of air fryer with cooking spray. Preheat air fryer to 380 F.
2 Lightly brush both sides of plantain slices with coconut oil. Sprinkle with brown sugar and jerk seasoning.
3 Working in two batches, cook in air fryer for 8 minutes until golden brown, turning once halfway through.
4 Remove and repeat for remaining slices. Let cool briefly before serving.

QUICK TIP

A ripe plantain is best when it's mostly black with just a little yellow— the perfect sweetness!

FANCY UP STORE-BOUGHT HUMMUS WITH A DRIZZLE OF GOOD OLIVE OIL AND SOME CRUSHED RED PEPPER.

Baked Pita Chips

BAKED PITA CHIPS

FAST FIX | PARTY FARE

Serve these chips on their own, with hummus or with various soft cheeses.

Start to finish 15 minutes
(10 minutes active)
Servings 4

2 pita bread rounds, cut into 6 triangles each
1 teaspoon lemon juice
1 teaspoon olive oil
½ teaspoon dried oregano
½ teaspoon salt
   Hummus

1 In a large bowl, add pita wedges. Add lemon juice, olive oil, oregano and salt and toss.
2 Put wedges in air fryer basket or racks (you may need to work in batches).
3 Cook at 400 F for 6 minutes, shaking occasionally, until browned.
4 Serve with hummus or your favorite chip dip.

MINI PEPPERONI PIZZAS

COMFORT FOOD | EASY | KID-FRIENDLY

Serve these little bites as an afterschool snack.

Start to finish 14 minutes
(10 minutes active)
Servings 16

   Vegetable cooking spray
1 (8-ounce) can refrigerated biscuits
2 tablespoons all-purpose flour
1 cup marinara sauce
1 cup shredded mozzarella cheese
4 ounces mini pepperoni slices
   GARNISHES Basil leaves, red pepper flakes, grated Parmesan

1 Preheat air fryer to 400 F.
2 Spray air fryer basket or tray with vegetable cooking spray.
3 Separate each biscuit into 2 layers. Dust with flour. Using a rolling pin, roll each biscuit half into a 3-inch circle.
4 Spread 2 teaspoons marinara sauce on each circle. Top with cheese and pepperoni.
5 Place pizzas in air fryer basket or rack (you will need to work in batches). Cook 4 minutes or until golden brown.
6 Place on a wire rack; repeat with remaining pizzas. Serve immediately; garnish as desired.

QUICK TIP

For a nontraditional take, try Brussels sprouts and a balsamic glaze or butternut squash and caramelized onions.

Cook's Notes

These pizzas are fun to customize! Make them a meat-lover's dream with **leftover sausage** or **meatball crumbles**, or go veggie by adding sauteed mushrooms, olives and/ or bell peppers.

SERVE CRUSHED RED PEPPER ON THE SIDE SO EVERYONE CAN ADD THE DESIRED AMOUNT OF HEAT.

Mini Pepperoni Pizzas

Sriracha
Cauliflower
Bites

SERVE THIS YOGURT
SAUCE ON THE SIDE AS
A DIPPING SAUCE IF
SOME OF YOUR GUESTS
ARE DAIRY-FREE.

SRIRACHA CAULIFLOWER BITES

CROWD-PLEASER | FAMILY FAVORITE

Vitamin-packed, low-carb cauliflower is also high in fiber and cooks quickly in the air fryer. Seasoning it with spicy Sriracha makes it extra tasty!

Start to finish 25 minutes
(10 minutes active)
Servings 4

3	cups cauliflower florets
1½	tablespoons canola oil
4	tablespoons Sriracha sauce
	Salt and freshly ground black pepper, to taste
2	tablespoons white rice flour or cornstarch
	Cooking spray
3	tablespoons plain yogurt
1	tablespoon lemon juice

1 Preheat air fryer to 400 F.
2 In a mixing bowl, toss cauliflower florets with oil, Sriracha and a generous pinch of salt and pepper.
3 Sprinkle with rice flour or cornstarch, tossing to coat. Arrange in basket and coat with cooking spray.
4 Cook for 15 minutes, shaking every 5 minutes, until cauliflower is crisp and golden brown at the edges.
5 Meanwhile, in a small bowl, stir together yogurt, lemon juice and a splash of hot water to thin. Season to taste with salt and pepper.
6 Transfer cauliflower to a serving plate; spoon over the yogurt dressing before serving.

SOFT PRETZELS

EASY | FAMILY FAVORITE

This beloved snack is easy to find in any grocery store in its hard version—but nothing beats warm soft pretzels! Try them with obatzda, a buttery, cheesy Bavarian dip that's traditionally served at Oktoberfest.

THESE PRETZELS ARE DELICIOUS PLAIN—BUT EVEN BETTER DIPPED IN MUSTARD OR MELTED CHEESE!

Soft Pretzels

Start to finish 30 minutes
(15 minutes active)
Servings 4

1	crescent dough sheet
	All-purpose flour, for dusting
½	cup water, at room temperature
	Coarse kosher salt
	Cooking spray

1 On a lightly floured surface, roll out dough into an 8x6-inch rectangle.
2 Using a sharp knife, cut out eight 1-inch-wide strips. Roll dough strips into ropes before shaping into pretzels, twisting and sealing ends of dough to complete.
3 Brush with water and sprinkle with salt.
4 Preheat air fryer to 330 F. Coat basket with cooking spray before arranging half the pretzels in basket. Leave space between pretzels; they will puff up as they bake.
5 Bake for 6–8 minutes until golden and cooked through. Remove to a baking rack to cool.
6 Repeat for remaining pretzels.

THAI-STYLE EGG ROLLS

CROWD-PLEASER | FAST FIX

Most grocery stores carry egg roll wrappers, so it's easier than ever to make these treats at home.

Start to finish 25 minutes
(15 minutes active)
Servings 6

- 1 pound rotisserie chicken, shredded
- ⅔ cup Thai peanut sauce, plus extra for serving
- 6 egg roll wrappers
- 2 medium carrots, peeled and very thinly sliced
- 1 red bell pepper, cored, seeded and julienned
- 3 scallions, chopped
  Cooking spray, or 1 tablespoon sesame oil

1 Preheat air fryer to 390 F. In a mixing bowl, toss chicken with peanut sauce.
2 Lay out egg roll wrappers on a clean surface and arrange a mixture of carrots, red pepper and scallions across bottom third of wrappers.
3 Spoon dressed chicken on top. Wet edges of wrappers with a damp fingertip before folding sides inward and then rolling up tightly. Coat egg rolls all over with cooking spray or brush with sesame oil.
4 Arrange in basket of air fryer and cook for 9–10 minutes until golden brown and crisp at the edges, turning once halfway through cooking.
5 Remove from air fryer when ready and let cool briefly before serving with additional peanut sauce on the side for dipping.

⌄
QUICK TIP

Make sure you completely seal the edges of each egg roll before placing them into the air fryer so they don't leak.

Cook's Notes

You can stuff almost anything into an egg roll wrapper. Keep it in the traditional Asian flavor of **pork, cabbage and bean sprouts**; give it a southwestern or Indian filling; or even make it a sweet treat, such as the Blueberry Pie Egg Rolls (page 135)!

Parmesan Popcorn

PARMESAN POPCORN

EASY | KID-FRIENDLY

When you are popping corn in the air fryer, first line the sides of the tray with foil or parchment. That way, the popped corn doesn't escape the basket and fly around the air fryer.

Start to finish 20 minutes
(5 minutes active)
Servings 6 cups

- 3 tablespoons popcorn kernels
- 1 tablespoon peanut oil
- 1 tablespoon sea salt
- ¼ cup grated Parmesan cheese

1 Add kernels to air fryer basket. Drizzle oil over kernels; toss to coat.
2 Cook at 400 F for 15 minutes, checking occasionally to prevent burning.
3 Remove popcorn and sprinkle with salt and Parmesan.

COCONUT SHRIMP

CROWD-PLEASER | FAST FIX

Panko breadcrumbs mixed with coconut give these shrimp the perfect amount of crunch.

Start to finish 25 minutes
(10 minutes active)
Servings 4

- ½ cup cornstarch
- 2 eggs, beaten with 1 tablespoon water
- 1½ cups panko breadcrumbs Salt and freshly ground black pepper, to taste
- ½ cup shredded coconut (see Quick Tip, right)
- 12 raw shrimp, deveined, tails on Cooking spray

1 Preheat air fryer to 350 F.
2 Place cornstarch, beaten eggs and breadcrumbs in three separate shallow dishes. Season each with salt and pepper and stir coconut into breadcrumbs.
3 Dust shrimp in cornstarch, shaking off excess. Dip into beaten eggs, turning to coat, and then dredge in coconut breadcrumbs to coat.
4 Coat basket with cooking spray. Arrange shrimp in basket in a single layer (you may need to work in batches).
5 Cook for 10–12 minutes until golden and crisp, turning about halfway through cooking.
6 Remove from air fryer and let cool briefly before serving.

QUICK TIP

Sweetened or unsweetened coconut? We prefer sweetened if the shrimp will be served plain, and unsweetened if you've got a sweet dipping sauce.

SWEET THAI CHILI
SAUCE, MIXED WITH
ORANGE MARMALADE,
MAKES A DELICIOUS
DIPPING SAUCE.

Coconut Shrimp

49

Cook's Notes

You can use many fruits to make air fryer chips. **Pears work well, as do green bananas.** To get the slices super thin, use a mandoline. They're not expensive, and they make slim, even slices a breeze.

Cinnamon Sugar Apple Chips

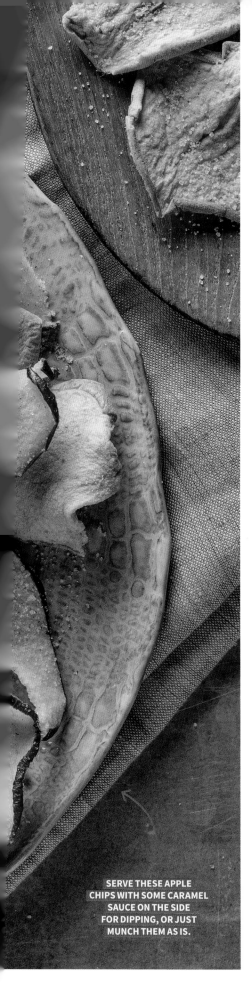

Loaded Potato Skins With Avocado

CINNAMON SUGAR APPLE CHIPS

EASY | HEALTHY | KID-FRIENDLY

Air frying your sliced apples makes for an addictive (and healthy!) snack. Honeycrisp apples have an ideal mix of sweetness and tartness for these chips.

Start to finish 20 minutes
(10 minutes active)
Servings 4

- 4 Honeycrisp apples, cored
- 1 tablespoon sugar
- 1 teaspoon ground cinnamon
  Cooking spray

1 Preheat air fryer to 400 F.
2 Cut apples into ⅛-inch slices.
3 In a small bowl, mix sugar and cinnamon; lightly sprinkle apple slices with mixture.
4 Coat air fryer basket with cooking spray. Place apples in a single layer in basket (you may need to work in batches). Cook for 4 minutes and flip, cooking for another 4 minutes. Place on a wire rack.
5 Store any leftovers in an airtight container.

LOADED POTATO SKINS WITH AVOCADO

FAMILY FAVORITE | PARTY FARE

Russet potatoes work well in this recipe: Their skins are strong, so they won't break or peel.

Start to finish 20 minutes
(5 minutes active)
Servings 8

- 4 boiled and cooled russet potatoes, halved
- ½ cup grated cheddar cheese
- ½ cup sour cream
- 2 scallions, sliced
- 1 cup chopped avocado
- 1 jalapeño, sliced

1 Scoop out most of the inside of the potatoes, leaving a potato skin "boat." Save the insides for another dish, such as mashed potatoes.
2 Place skins inside air fryer basket or racks. Top with cheese and cook at 325 F for 5 minutes or until cheese is melted (you may need to work in batches).
3 Remove from air fryer and top with sour cream, scallions, chopped avocado and sliced jalapeño.
4 Serve immediately.

51

Stuffed Olives

CHICKEN MEATBALLS

FAST FIX | PARTY FARE

Ground chicken provides a healthy, lean protein source in this easy dish. Make a few batches ahead of time and freeze them for those nights when you don't feel like cooking from scratch.

Start to finish 25 minutes
(10 minutes active)
Servings 4

1	pound ground chicken
1	egg
½	cup Parmesan cheese, grated
½	cup plain breadcrumbs, plus extra for rolling
1	garlic clove, finely chopped
1	teaspoon dried rosemary
1	teaspoon salt
½	teaspoon freshly ground black pepper
	Cooking spray
	GARNISH Rosemary sprigs

1 In a large mixing bowl, stir together chicken, egg, Parmesan, breadcrumbs, garlic, rosemary, salt and pepper.
2 Divide and shape into meatballs, rolling in additional breadcrumbs to coat. Preheat air fryer to 400 F.
3 Coat basket with cooking spray. Place meatballs in basket in a single layer (you may need to work in batches).
4 Coat meatballs with cooking spray. Cook for 12 minutes, turning once halfway through cooking time.
5 Cook remaining meatballs in same manner.
6 Serve warm, threaded onto rosemary sprigs, if desired.

QUICK TIP

Try these meatballs with ground turkey instead of chicken, or use a mix of ground meats such as beef and pork.

STUFFED OLIVES

CROWD-PLEASER | FAST FIX

Olives have been cultivated since at least 3000 B.C.—it seems the ancient Greeks found them as delicious as we do! Their addictive saltiness makes them a popular finger food, and they're also full of heart-healthy fat. Our version—stuffed and air fried—makes them a perfect cocktail party snack, especially served with meats and cheeses.

Start to finish 30 minutes
(10 minutes active)
Servings 4

1	cup pitted green olives (manzanilla olives are a good choice for stuffing)
4	anchovy fillets, in oil, drained and chopped
¾	cup plain breadcrumbs
½	cup all-purpose flour
1	egg
	Cooking spray
	Salt and freshly ground black pepper, to taste

1 Preheat air fryer to 350 F.
2 Using the tip of a small knife, carefully stuff olives with chopped anchovies.
3 Place breadcrumbs, flour and egg in separate shallow dishes, seasoning each with salt and pepper. Beat egg thoroughly in a separate bowl.
4 Toss olives in seasoned flour, shaking off excess. Dip into egg, turning to coat, and then dredge in breadcrumbs to coat.
5 Coat air fryer basket with cooking spray. Arrange olives in basket in a single layer and coat with cooking spray.
6 Cook for 12–15 minutes, gently shaking basket occasionally, until golden and crisp.
7 Remove from air fryer and let cool briefly before serving.

Cook's Notes

The **rosemary** in these meatballs adds a sharp, woodsy flavor, so a cool **yogurt dipping sauce** or **marinara sauce** are both good complements. Serve sauces on the side so guests can spoon on as much as they'd like.

Chicken Meatballs

Cook's Notes

A snack such as these spiced nuts is **healthy in moderation (especially when prepared in an air fryer).** Almonds are high in protein and antioxidants; walnuts provide omega-3 fatty acids; cashews are loaded with essential vitamins and minerals.

Spiced Mixed Nuts

SPICED MIXED NUTS

CLASSIC | EASY | PARTY FARE

Sweet and spicy, these nuts are delicious with mixed drinks at a cocktail party.

Start to finish 25 minutes
(5 minutes active)
Servings 4

- 1 teaspoon ground cinnamon
- 1 teaspoon sugar
- ¼ teaspoon cayenne pepper
- 1 egg white
- 1 cup mixed nuts

1 Preheat air fryer to 300 F.
2 In a small bowl, mix cinnamon, sugar and cayenne pepper. Set aside.
3 In another small bowl, beat egg white, then toss with nuts.
4 Toss nuts in spice mixture to coat.
5 Place mixture in air fryer basket and cook for 10 minutes. Stir, then cook for another 10 minutes.
6 Let nuts cool completely before serving. Store in an airtight container.

Oyster Cracker
Snack Mix

OYSTER CRACKER SNACK MIX

EASY | PARTY FARE

These addictive seasoned crackers will be a party favorite for sure! Of course, they're also delicious tossed into soups, chili or as salad toppers.

Start to finish 15 minutes
(5 minutes active)
Servings 6

- 3 tablespoons canola oil
- 3 tablespoons Worcestershire sauce
- 1 tablespoon lemon juice
- 1 tablespoon garlic powder
- 1 tablespoon onion powder
- 1 teaspoon celery salt
- 1 (9-ounce) bag oyster crackers
- 2 tablespoons grated Parmesan cheese

1 Combine oil and next 5 ingredients. Toss in crackers and coat with mixture.
2 Add crackers to air fryer basket or racks (you may need to work in batches).
3 Cook at 325 F for 10 minutes, shaking every 2 minutes.
4 Remove from air fryer and cool. Store in airtight container.

RANCH PARTY MIX

EASY | KID-FRIENDLY | PARTY FARE

The popular snack gets a major flavor boost when it's cooked in an air fryer.

Start to finish 10 minutes
(5 minutes active)
Servings 8

- 2 cups crisp wheat cereal squares
- 2 cups crisp rice cereal squares
- 2 cups goldfish crackers
- 2 cups pretzel sticks
- ¼ cup butter, melted
- 1 (1-ounce) packet ranch dressing seasoning
- ½ teaspoon cayenne pepper

1 Preheat air fryer to 350 F.
2 In a large bowl, toss wheat cereal, rice cereal, goldfish crackers and pretzel sticks.
3 In a small bowl, mix butter, ranch mix and cayenne pepper. Drizzle over snack mix; stir to coat evenly.
4 Place snack mix in basket or tray of air fryer (you may need to work in batches). Cook for 5 minutes.
5 Let cool before serving. Store in an airtight container.

SEE
P.58

Rib-Eye Steak

SAVORY
MEATS

WHETHER IT'S A SIMPLE STEAK OR FUN FARE SUCH AS CORN DOGS, YOU'LL FIND SOMETHING TO STICK TO YOUR RIBS WITH THESE HEARTY RECIPES.

RIB-EYE STEAK

FAMILY FAVORITE | FAST FIX

These juicy steaks are so flavorful, all they need is your favorite peppercorn sauce on the side.

Start to finish 30 minutes
(15 minutes active)
Servings 4

- 2 **rib-eye steaks, about 8 ounces each, trimmed**
  Cooking spray
- 2 **tablespoons canola oil**
  Flaked sea salt
  Freshly ground black pepper
- 2 **rosemary sprigs**

1 Let steaks stand at room temperature for 15 minutes.
2 Preheat air fryer to 400 F. Coat basket with cooking spray.
3 Rub steaks with canola oil and liberally season with salt and pepper.
4 Place steaks in basket and cook for 6 minutes. Turn steaks and top with rosemary sprigs before cooking another 6 minutes for medium steaks; adjust cooking time by 1–2 minutes more or less for your preferred degree of doneness.
5 Remove from basket and let rest, covered loosely with foil, for at least 5 minutes.
6 Cut into thin slices and serve with a sprinkle of salt.

JERK PORK SKEWERS

FAST FIX | PARTY FARE

Jerk seasoning is complex and aromatic, containing both sweet and spicy notes.

Start to finish 20 minutes
(14 minutes active)
Servings 4

- ¼ **cup jerk seasoning powder**
- 1 **(1-pound) pork tenderloin, cubed**
- 4 **bamboo skewers, soaked in water for 20 minutes**
  Black bean salsa
  GARNISH **Cilantro sprigs**

1 Sprinkle jerk seasoning on pork cubes. Thread pork cubes on skewers.
2 Place skewers in air fryer basket or racks.
3 Cook at 350 F for 6 minutes or until temperature reaches 145 F on thermometer.
4 Serve with black bean salsa and garnish with cilantro, if desired.

COUNTRY-STYLE RIBS

CROWD-PLEASER | FAMILY FAVORITE

Country-style ribs are meatier than most other cuts of ribs. Serve them with sides of baked beans, potato salad and cornbread—and napkins!

Start to finish 25 minutes (5 minutes active)
Servings 4

- 1 **pound boneless country-style pork ribs**
- 1 **tablespoon olive oil**
- 3 **tablespoons barbecue rub seasoning**
- 1 **cup barbecue sauce, warmed**

1 Brush ribs with oil. Sprinkle barbecue rub on both sides of ribs.
2 Place ribs in air fryer basket or racks and cook at 350 F for 18–20 minutes, turning them halfway through.
3 Remove from air fryer and brush with barbecue sauce to serve.

⌄⌄ QUICK TIP

Cooking times can vary widely depending on the air fryer model you are using, so err on the earlier side to check if the meat is prepared to your liking.

Sizzling Steak With Herb Butter

Cook's Notes

With the popularity of keto diets these days, it's no surprise that compound butter—butter mixed with herbs and other seasonings—is a favorite steak topping. Some other herbs that work well include **basil, rosemary and thyme.**

SIZZLING STEAK WITH HERB BUTTER

CLASSIC | FAMILY FAVORITE

A strip steak works well with this recipe. It's tender and flavorful.

Start to finish 20 minutes (5 minutes active)
Servings 2

¼	**cup butter, softened**
1	**teaspoon chopped parsley**
1	**teaspoon minced garlic**
1	**teaspoon ground black pepper, divided**
2	**(8-ounce) strip steaks**
1	**teaspoon salt**
	Cooking spray

1 In a small bowl, mix butter, parsley, garlic and half of the pepper until well combined.
2 Season steaks on both sides with salt and remaining pepper.
3 Coat air fryer basket or rack with cooking spray. Place steaks in basket.
4 Cook at 400 F for 6 minutes, flipping steaks halfway through.
5 Remove steaks from air fryer and allow to rest for 10 minutes; place on serving plates and top with herb butter.

Bacon Cheeseburger Deluxe

BACON CHEESEBURGER DELUXE

CROWD-PLEASER | FAST FIX

Seasoned beef makes these burgers extra savory, and once you pile on the toppings, we're sure they'll become a go-to dish for busy nights.

Start to finish 25 minutes
(10 minutes active)
Servings 4

1½	**pounds 80% lean ground beef**
2	**tablespoons barbecue sauce**
1	**teaspoon kosher salt**
½	**teaspoon freshly ground black pepper**
½	**teaspoon garlic powder**
½	**teaspoon onion powder**
4	**bacon slices, cut in half**
4	**slices American or Colby-Jack cheese**
4	**sesame seed rolls, split**
4	**large bibb lettuce leaves, washed**
	Ketchup
1	**beefsteak tomato, thinly sliced**
1	**white onion, thinly sliced**

1 Preheat air fryer to 370 F. Pour a little water into bottom of air fryer basket.
2 In a mixing bowl, mix together ground beef, barbecue sauce, salt, pepper, garlic powder and onion powder.
3 Use hands to divide and shape into 4 patties; make a thumb imprint in center of each patty to help patties keep their shape when frying. Place patties in basket in a single layer.
4 Cook for 10 minutes. Flip and place 2 half-slices of bacon on each patty. Cook for an additional 6–10 minutes (6 minutes if you want a rare burger, up to 10 for well-done).
5 Remove bacon from patties and keep warm wrapped in foil. Top each patty with a slice of cheese, then return them to air fryer for another minute or until melted.
6 When ready to assemble, place lettuce on bottom halves of buns. Place patties on top; spread with ketchup.
7 Top with tomato, onion and bacon. Put on the tops of buns before serving.

Italian Pork Chops With Marinara

ITALIAN PORK CHOPS WITH MARINARA

FAMILY FAVORITE | PARTY FARE

These pork chops are moist, crisp and perfectly delicious. The light breading helps keep the pork juicy.

Start to finish 28 minutes
(10 minutes active)
Servings 4

Cooking spray
4 (6-ounce) bone-in pork chops
½ teaspoon kosher salt
½ teaspoon ground black pepper
½ teaspoon garlic powder
1 egg
½ cup grated Parmesan cheese
½ cup seasoned Italian breadcrumbs
2 tablespoons chopped Italian parsley
½ cup shredded mozzarella cheese
1 cup marinara sauce
GARNISH Basil leaves

1 Preheat air fryer to 380 F. Coat basket or tray with cooking spray.
2 Season pork chops with salt, pepper and garlic powder.
3 In a shallow bowl, beat egg.
4 In a medium bowl, mix together Parmesan, breadcrumbs and parsley.
5 Dip each chop in egg, then dredge in breadcrumb mixture, coating completely. Lightly coat both sides of each chop with cooking spray.
6 Place chops in basket; cook 8 to 12 minutes, flipping after 6 minutes. Top with cheese; cook 2 more minutes.
7 Garnish and serve hot with individual portions of marinara sauce on the side.

STATE FAIR CORN DOGS

KID-FRIENDLY | PARTY FARE

Use any kind of hot dog you like (even veggie) for this fun treat.

Start to finish 25 minutes
(15 minutes active)
Servings 4

4 hot dogs
1 cup flour
2 eggs
1½ cups finely ground cornflakes
Cooking spray
GARNISHES Mustard, ketchup, mayonnaise

1 Insert a skewer or long ice cream stick into each hot dog.
2 In a shallow dish, add flour. In a second dish, beat eggs. In a third dish, add cornflakes.
3 Roll each hot dog in flour and shake off excess, then dip in egg, then dredge in cornflakes.
4 Coat air fryer basket or rack with cooking spray.
5 Place corn dogs in basket. Cook at 375 F for 10 minutes, turning after 5 minutes.
6 Serve with garnishes on the side.

Cook's Notes

Add even more fun to this carnival classic: **Try mixing a bit of paprika or other seasoning into the cornflakes;** use breakfast sausage links for a morning treat; or go for Italian sausage and mix some Parmesan with the cornflakes.

Classic Steak Fajitas

COLORFUL BELL PEPPER STRIPS ADD FLAVOR—AND VITAMINS—TO A STEAMING PLATE OF FAJITA FIXINGS.

CLASSIC STEAK FAJITAS

EASY | FAMILY FAVORITE | KID-FRIENDLY

With the toppings on the side, everyone gets a custom meal.

Start to finish 15 minutes
(5 minutes active)
Servings 4

Cooking spray
3 tablespoons vegetable oil
½ teaspoon chili powder
1 teaspoon cumin
1 teaspoon garlic powder
1 teaspoon salt
½ teaspoon ground black pepper
1 pound flank steak, sliced
1 red bell pepper, sliced
1 green bell pepper, sliced
1 yellow bell pepper, sliced
1 white onion, sliced
8 flour tortillas, warmed
 GARNISHES Guacamole, salsa, sour cream, sliced scallions

1 Preheat air fryer to 390 F. Line basket with foil; coat with cooking spray.
2 In a large bowl, combine oil, chili powder, cumin, garlic powder, salt and pepper. Add steak slices, peppers and onions. Toss to coat.
3 Pour meat mixture into air fryer basket and cook for 5 minutes; prepare in batches if needed.
4 Serve with warmed tortillas and assorted garnishes on the side.

LAMB CHOPS WITH MINT JELLY

CLASSIC | PARTY FARE

Dijon mustard seasons these lamb chops to perfection and provides a nice contrast to the sweet mint jelly.

Start to finish 20 minutes (5 minutes active)
Servings 4

Cooking spray
2 tablespoons Dijon mustard
1 teaspoon olive oil
1 teaspoon chopped mint
1 tablespoon lemon juice
½ teaspoon salt
½ teaspoon ground black pepper
8 loin lamb chops
 Mint jelly, for serving

1 Preheat air fryer to 390 F. Coat basket or tray with cooking spray.
2 In a small bowl, combine mustard, olive oil, mint, lemon juice, salt and pepper.
3 Brush mustard-herb mixture over all sides of lamb chops.
4 Place lamb chops in prepared basket or tray. Cook for 15 minutes, flipping after 8 minutes.
5 Serve with mint jelly.

SAUSAGE CALZONES

EASY | FAMILY FAVORITE

Store-bought pizza dough isn't just for pizzas! These little handheld treats put it to perfect use.

Start to finish 20 minutes
(15 minutes active)
Servings 8

1 (13.8-ounce) can refrigerated pizza dough
¼ cup pizza sauce
3 tablespoons diced red onion
⅓ cup cooked Italian sausage
¼ cup shredded mozzarella
 Marinara sauce, for serving

1 On a floured surface, roll out pizza dough. Using a cookie cutter or large drinking glass, cut dough into eight 3-inch circles.
2 Place pizza sauce, onion, sausage and mozzarella on one side of dough rounds. Do not overfill.
3 Fold over into half-moon shape and seal edges with tines of a fork.
4 Place calzones in air fryer basket or rack (you may need to cook in batches).
5 Cook at 400 F for 6 minutes or until browned.
6 Serve with marinara sauce.

Brat Hoagies

1 Top the mini naan with barbecue sauce, pork, onion and cheese.
2 Coat air fryer basket or rack with cooking spray. Place pizza in basket.
3 Cook at 375 F for 5–7 minutes or until cheese is melted. Add garnishes and serve.

PORK CHOPS WITH APPLESAUCE

COMFORT FOOD | EASY

No matter how busy your day, you can still have a hot, home-cooked meal—it takes just minutes with an air fryer. Try these pork chops with some roasted fingerling potatoes.

Start to finish 15 minutes (2 minutes active)
Servings 4

Cooking spray
4   bone-in pork loin chops
½   teaspoon salt
½   teaspoon ground black pepper
Applesauce, for serving
GARNISH Thyme sprigs

1 Preheat air fryer to 400 F. Coat basket or tray with cooking spray.
2 Sprinkle pork chops with salt and pepper.
3 Place chops in basket or tray. Cook for 12 minutes, flipping halfway through cooking time, or until a thermometer inserted in meat registers 145 F.
4 Serve with applesauce and garnish with thyme sprigs, if desired.

BRAT HOAGIES

EASY | PARTY FARE

A smear of spicy mustard is all this delicious sandwich needs, so the flavors in the bratwurst can stand out.

Start to finish 20 minutes (5 minutes active)
Servings 2

1   small onion, sliced
1   small green bell pepper, sliced
    Cooking spray
2   precooked brats
    Spicy mustard, for serving
2   hoagie or hot dog rolls

1 Place onion and peppers on a foil sheet. Coat with cooking spray; fold up and seal edges to make a packet.
2 Place packet and brats in air fryer basket or racks and cook at 350 F for 15 minutes. Remove from air fryer.

3 Spread mustard on rolls. Place brats in rolls; top with onion and peppers.

BARBECUE PULLED PORK INDIVIDUAL PIZZA

EASY | FAMILY FAVORITE

Many grocery stores carry pulled pork in barbecue sauce to use in sandwiches—or as a pizza topping, as we do here. You can also use any leftovers you've got in the fridge.

Start to finish 10 minutes (3 minutes active)
Servings 1

1   mini naan bread (or pita)
2   tablespoons barbecue sauce
¼   cup pulled pork
1   tablespoon chopped red onion
2   tablespoons shredded mozzarella
    Cooking spray
GARNISHES Coleslaw, dill pickle slices

QUICK TIP

Bratwurst is loaded with unique flavors, such as sage, nutmeg and ginger, making it ideal for a simple preparation such as these tasty sandwiches.

Pork Chops
With Applesauce

ROASTED ROOT
VEGETABLES MAKE
A PORK CHOP
DINNER FEEL EVEN
HEARTIER.

GREEK MEATBALLS WITH TZATZIKI

EASY | PARTY FARE

A lamb and beef blend makes these cocktail-size meatballs extra flavorful and moist. You can also sub in ground turkey or pork—but lamb is more in keeping with the Greek flavors.

Start to finish 27 minutes
(15 minutes active)
Servings 8

	Cooking spray
1	**pound ground lamb**
1	**pound ground beef**
1	**egg, beaten**
1	**tablespoon dried oregano**
1	**tablespoon dried dill**
1	**tablespoon lemon juice**
1½	**teaspoons sea salt**
1	**teaspoon ground black pepper**
	Tzatziki, for serving
	GARNISH Oregano leaves

1 Preheat air fryer to 350 F. Coat basket or tray with cooking spray.
2 In a large bowl, combine lamb, beef, egg, oregano, dill, lemon juice, salt and pepper; mix well.
3 Form mixture into 1-inch balls.
4 Place meatballs in prepared basket or tray (you may need to work in batches) and cook for 7 minutes. Shake meatballs and cook 4 additional minutes.
5 Allow to cool 2 to 3 minutes. Garnish and serve with tzatziki.

≫
QUICK TIP

Tzatziki also makes a tangy dip for pita chips or cutup vegetables. You can find it in most grocery stores; there are even nondairy, plant-based versions.

Pork Schnitzel

PORK SCHNITZEL

CLASSIC | FAMILY FAVORITE

"Schnitzel" means cutlet or scallop in German, so you'll want to make sure your pork chops are sliced evenly thin (you can do it yourself, or ask your butcher to do it for you).

Start to finish 25 minutes
(10 minutes active)
Servings 4

- ½ cup flour
- ½ teaspoon salt
- ½ teaspoon ground black pepper
- 1 egg
- ⅔ cup seasoned panko breadcrumbs
- ½ teaspoon Old Bay seasoning
- Cooking spray
- 4 boneless pork chops, pounded to ⅓-inch thick

1 In one shallow bowl, mix flour, salt and pepper. In a second bowl, beat egg. In a third bowl, mix panko and Old Bay seasoning.
2 Dip each chop in flour mixture to coat; shake off excess and dip into egg, then dredge in panko mixture.
3 Coat air fryer basket or rack with cooking spray.
4 Place chops in air fryer and cook at 400 F for 12–14 minutes, turning after 8 minutes.
5 Check the temperature of the pork with a thermometer. Make sure it reads 145 F, or continue to cook them until it reaches that temperature.

BEEF AND BLACK BEAN EMPANADAS

CLASSIC | FAMILY FAVORITE

These flaky, savory pastries originated as handheld snacks, but they're hearty enough to be the star of a meal.

Start to finish 28 minutes
(20 minutes active)
Servings 6

USE A FORK TO POKE HOLES IN THE DOUGH BEFORE YOU COOK THE EMPANADAS SO STEAM CAN ESCAPE AND THE PASTRY DOESN'T SPLIT AT THE EDGES.

Beef and Black Bean Empanadas

- Cooking spray
- 1 tablespoon olive oil
- ½ cup chopped white onion
- 1 teaspoon minced garlic
- 1 pound ground beef
- 1 cup cooked black beans
- 1 cup tomato sauce
- ½ teaspoon kosher salt
- ¼ teaspoon ground black pepper
- ½ teaspoon onion powder
- ½ teaspoon ground paprika
- ½ teaspoon ground cumin
- 2 tablespoons chopped cilantro
- 1 (14.1-ounce) package refrigerated pie crusts
- Guacamole and red pepper flakes, for serving

1 Preheat air fryer to 330 F. Coat basket or tray with cooking spray.

2 In a large skillet, add oil, onion and garlic. Saute for 5 minutes. Add in beef and cook 5 more minutes. Drain fat.
3 Add black beans, tomato sauce, salt, pepper, onion powder, paprika, cumin and cilantro. Stir and cook 2 minutes.
4 Unroll pastry on floured cutting board. Using a 4-inch round cookie cutter, cut rounds from dough. Re-roll dough scraps to cut additional rounds.
5 Place 2 or 3 teaspoons of beef mixture in center of each round. Wet edges of each round with water; fold each round in half and press edges with fork to seal.
6 Set a single layer of empanadas into prepared basket or tray (you may need to work in batches).
7 Cook for 8 minutes, until slightly browned. Serve warm with guacamole and red pepper flakes.

Country-Fried Steak

Cooking spray

⅓	cup all-purpose flour
⅓	cup cornstarch
2	teaspoons Chinese five-spice powder
1	teaspoon salt
½	teaspoon ground black pepper
1	egg
2	tablespoons milk
1	pound boneless pork, cut into 1-inch cubes
1½	cups large chunks mixed red, green and yellow bell peppers
½	cup ketchup
2	tablespoons rice wine vinegar
2	tablespoons brown sugar
¼	cup orange juice
1	tablespoon soy sauce
1	teaspoon minced garlic
1	cup cubed pineapple
	Cooked white rice
	GARNISH Sliced scallions

COUNTRY-FRIED STEAK

CLASSIC | FAMILY FAVORITE

Sometimes called chicken-fried steak, this dish is often served with a creamy, milk-based gravy on the side, but it's delicious with any gravy you like.

Start to finish 25 minutes
(15 minutes active)
Servings 4

1	cup flour
1	teaspoon salt
1	teaspoon ground black pepper
1	teaspoon garlic powder
1	teaspoon onion powder
1	cup buttermilk
1	teaspoon hot sauce
1	egg
4	(6-ounce) cube steaks
	Cooking spray
	Gravy

1 In a shallow bowl, combine flour, salt, pepper, garlic powder and onion powder. In a second shallow bowl, beat buttermilk, hot sauce and egg.
2 Dredge steaks in the seasoned flour mixture, shaking off any excess.
3 Dredge in the buttermilk mixture, allowing access to drip off.
4 Dredge in the flour mixture again, shaking off excess.
5 Place breaded steaks in air fryer basket or racks. Lightly coat with cooking spray.
6 Cook at 400 F for 8 minutes, turning halfway through the cooking process.
7 Remove from air fryer. Serve with gravy on the side.

SWEET AND SOUR PORK

CLASSIC | EASY | FAMILY FAVORITE

Pork stays juicy and tender in the air fryer version of the beloved Chinese takeout dish.

Start to finish 30 minutes
(15 minutes active)
Servings 4

1 Preheat air fryer to 400 F. Coat basket or tray with cooking spray.
2 In a shallow bowl, combine flour, cornstarch, five-spice powder, salt and pepper. In a second bowl, beat egg and milk.
3 Dredge pork cubes in flour mixture, then dip in egg, then dredge them again in flour mixture to coat well. Set aside.
4 Coat bell peppers with cooking spray, place in basket or tray and cook 5 minutes, shaking halfway through.
5 Meanwhile, in a medium saucepan over medium heat, mix ketchup, vinegar, brown sugar, orange juice, soy sauce and garlic; bring to a boil. Reduce heat; simmer for 5 minutes.
6 Add bell peppers and pineapple chunks to saucepan. Simmer for an additional 2 minutes. Set aside and keep warm.
7 Coat pork cubes with cooking spray. Add pork to basket or tray and cook for 6 minutes, shaking basket halfway through.
8 Add cooked pork to saucepan; stir to coat. Divide rice among serving plates, top with pork, garnish and serve.

Cook's Notes

Five-spice powder, used to season this pork, is an aromatic blend usually comprised of **fennel seeds, cinnamon, cloves, Sichuan pepper and star anise.** It works particularly well with fattier meats, such as pork, and can be found in most grocery stores.

Sweet and Sour Pork

DELICIOUS
POULTRY

MAKING CHICKEN AND TURKEY IN THE
AIR FRYER MEANS THESE FAVORITES
COME OUT PERFECT EVERY TIME!

CHUNKS OF FRESH VEGGIES ADD COLOR AND NUTRITIONAL BENEFITS TO ANY SAVORY DISH.

Cook's Notes

If you have leftover chimichangas, you can save them for a future quick lunch or dinner. Wrap them individually in **plastic wrap** and freeze. Defrost in the refrigerator, then pop them back in the air fryer, preheated to 320 F, for 3 to 5 minutes.

Chicken Chimichangas

SERVE THIS OVER
BROWN RICE
FOR EXTRA FIBER
AND VITAMINS.

GENERAL TSO'S CHICKEN

CLASSIC | EASY | FAMILY FAVORITE

The mouthwatering sauce is delicious on lots of other air fryer–cooked proteins, such as shrimp, beef or tofu.

Start to finish 30 minutes
(14 minutes active)
Servings 4

	Cooking spray
½	**cup chicken broth**
2	**tablespoons sesame oil**
2	**tablespoons soy sauce, divided**
1	**tablespoon hoisin sauce**
3	**tablespoons cornstarch, divided**
1	**teaspoon minced garlic**
1	**teaspoon Sriracha sauce**
1	**pound skinless, boneless chicken breasts, cut into bite-size pieces**
1	**teaspoon sliced scallions**
1	**teaspoon toasted sesame seeds**
1	**teaspoon black sesame seeds**

1 Preheat air fryer to 400 F. Coat basket or tray with cooking spray.

2 To make sauce, in a medium saucepan over medium heat, add broth, sesame oil, 1 tablespoon soy sauce, hoisin sauce, 1 tablespoon cornstarch, garlic and Sriracha. Whisk until cornstarch is dissolved. Raise heat to medium-high; bring to a boil. Reduce heat to low.

3 In a medium bowl, add chicken, remaining cornstarch and remaining soy sauce into a bowl; stir until chicken is evenly coated. Place chicken in prepared basket or tray.

4 Cook for 8 minutes, flip and spray undersides of chicken with more cooking spray. Cook about 8 minutes more.

5 In a large serving bowl, place chicken. Pour in sauce and toss to coat. Top with scallions and sesame seeds to serve.

QUICK TIP

Up the spiciness even more by adding in some red pepper flakes.

79

Nashville Hot
Chicken Sandwich

OPT FOR LARGER-THAN-
USUAL HAMBURGER
BUNS TO ACCOMMODATE
THE CHICKEN AND ALL
THE TOPPINGS.

powder, whisking until sugar dissolves and mixture is heated through.
7 Remove chicken from air fryer and place in a large bowl; add sauce and toss to coat. Place a piece of chicken on each bottom bun. Top with lettuce, tomato and pickles; replace top bun.

BANG BANG CHICKEN WITH HONEY-SRIRACHA SAUCE

EASY | FAMILY FAVORITE | KID-FRIENDLY

This dish got its name from the sound made as cooks tenderized the chicken with a stick. The popular American version is best known for its delectable, creamy sauce.

Start to finish 30 minutes
(15 minutes active)
Servings 4

- ½ cup mayonnaise
- 2 tablespoons honey
- 1 tablespoon plus 2 teaspoons Sriracha sauce, divided
  Cooking spray
- 1 cup buttermilk
- ⅔ cup all-purpose flour
- ½ cup cornstarch
- 1 egg
- ½ teaspoon salt
- ¼ teaspoon ground black pepper
- 1½ cups panko breadcrumbs
- 1 pound boneless, skinless chicken breast, cut into 1-inch pieces
  GARNISH **Parsley**

1 To make sauce, in a small bowl, whisk mayonnaise, honey and 1 tablespoon Sriracha. Set aside.
2 Preheat air fryer to 375 F. Coat basket or tray with cooking spray.
3 In a large bowl, mix buttermilk, flour, cornstarch, egg, remaining Sriracha, salt and pepper.
4 In a shallow dish, place breadcrumbs.
5 Working in batches, dip chicken pieces in buttermilk mixture, then in breadcrumbs. Place in air fryer.
6 Cook for 8 to 10 minutes, flipping halfway through cooking.
7 Garnish and serve sauce on the side.

NASHVILLE HOT CHICKEN SANDWICH

CLASSIC | COMFORT FOOD

There are several variations of this spicy Tennessee specialty, but they all include pickles!

Start to finish 30 minutes
(15 minutes active)
Servings 4

Cooking spray
- 1 cup buttermilk
- 2 eggs
- ½ cup plus 1 tablespoon hot wing sauce, divided
- 1 (5-ounce) box Louisiana Fish Fry Air Fryer Seasoned Coating Mix for Chicken
- 4 boneless, skinless chicken thighs
- 1 tablespoon brown sugar
- 1 teaspoon ground black pepper
- ½ teaspoon garlic powder
- 4 hamburger buns
- 1 cup shredded iceberg lettuce
- 8 tomato slices
  Dill pickle chips, for serving

1 Preheat air fryer to 400 F. Coat basket or tray with cooking spray.
2 In a shallow bowl, whisk together buttermilk, eggs and 1 tablespoon hot sauce. In a second shallow bowl, add seasoned coating mix.
3 Dip each chicken thigh in buttermilk mixture, then dredge in coating mix, pressing to adhere.
4 Coat thighs with cooking spray and place in prepared basket or tray.
5 Cook 14 to 16 minutes or until coating is crispy and chicken is cooked through.
6 While chicken cooks, in a small saucepan over low heat, stir remaining hot sauce, sugar, pepper and garlic

CHICKEN LO MEIN

CLASSIC | FAMILY FAVORITE

If you can't find precooked noodles, get the dry ones and cook them according to package directions first.

Start to finish 25 minutes
(10 minutes active)
Servings 2

 Cooking spray
2 boneless, skinless chicken breasts, cut into strips
½ teaspoon kosher salt
½ teaspoon red pepper flakes
1 yellow onion, sliced
1 cup matchstick-cut carrots
2 tablespoons soy sauce
1 (14.2-ounce) package precooked lo mein noodles
 GARNISH **Sliced scallions**

1 Preheat air fryer to 350 F. Coat basket or tray with cooking spray.
2 In a large bowl, toss chicken with salt and pepper flakes. Place in prepared basket or tray and cook for 6 minutes.
3 Add onion, carrots and soy sauce to basket and cook 6 minutes more. Stir in noodles and cook 1 minute more.
5 Garnish and serve.

Chicken Milanese
Over Arugula

CHICKEN MILANESE OVER ARUGULA

CLASSIC | PARTY FARE

The slight natural spiciness of the arugula nicely balances the crust on the chicken.

Start to finish 30 minutes
(15 minutes active)
Servings 6

 Cooking spray
⅓ cup all-purpose flour
1 teaspoon kosher salt, divided
½ teaspoon ground black pepper, divided
2 large eggs
1¼ cups panko breadcrumbs
¼ cup grated Parmigiano Reggiano cheese
1½ pounds boneless, skinless chicken cutlets
 Arugula, for serving
 GARNISH **Lemon wedges**

1 Preheat air fryer to 400 F. Coat basket or tray with cooking spray.
2 In a shallow bowl, place flour, ½ teaspoon salt and ¼ teaspoon pepper. In another shallow bowl, beat eggs, 1 teaspoon water and remaining salt and pepper. In a third shallow bowl, mix breadcrumbs and cheese.
3 Dredge each cutlet in flour, then dip in egg mixture, then dip in breadcrumb mixture, gently pressing into cutlet to adhere.
4 Coat cutlets on both sides with cooking spray.
5 Cook for 13 to 15 minutes, flipping halfway through, until chicken is cooked through and breading is crispy and browned.
6 Divide arugula among 6 serving plates; top with cutlets, garnish and serve.

QUICK TIP

Lightly toss the arugula in a simple vinaigrette of olive oil, balsamic vinegar and freshly cracked black pepper first for even more flavor.

Chicken
Fried Rice

Chicken
and Cheese
Quesadilla

CHICKEN FRIED RICE

EASY | KID-FRIENDLY

This flavorful dish can stand on its own as a main meal or work as a side dish with an Asian-inspired entrée.

Start to finish 15 minutes (5 minutes active)
Servings 4

Cooking spray
1 cup cooked chicken
4 cups cooked white rice
¼ cup diced onion
¼ cup diced carrots
¼ cup green peas
¼ cup soy sauce
Sriracha sauce, for serving

1 Place foil in air fryer basket, or put a pan on air fryer rack. Coat foil or pan with cooking spray.
2 In a large bowl, combine chicken and next 5 ingredients. Add mixture to basket or pan.
3 Cook at 400 F for 10 minutes, stirring halfway through cooking. Add additional soy sauce, if needed.
4 Serve with Sriracha on the side.

CHICKEN AND CHEESE QUESADILLA

EASY | FAMILY FAVORITE

Quesadillas go great with guacamole and a side of black beans, or spice them up with salsa.

Start to finish 15 minutes (5 minutes active)
Servings 4

Cooking spray
2 flour tortillas
⅓ cup Mexican-blend shredded cheese
½ cup cooked shredded chicken
GARNISH Chopped tomatoes

1 Coat tortillas on both sides with cooking spray.
2 Place 1 tortilla in air fryer basket or tray.
3 Sprinkle tortilla evenly with cheese and chicken. Place second tortilla on top.
4 Cook at 325 F for 6 to 9 minutes, carefully flipping the quesadilla over halfway through cooking.
5 Remove from air fryer and slice into wedges. Garnish and serve.

Gourmet
Chicken
Sandwich

CHICKEN CAESAR SALAD

CLASSIC | FAST FIX

Chunks of avocado may not be part of a traditional Caesar, but they add delicious, heart-healthy fats, plenty of fiber, and sweetness and creaminess to this salad.

Start to finish 30 minutes
(10 minutes active)
Servings 4

- 2 large chicken breasts, with skin
- ¼ cup olive oil, divided
- Salt
- Freshly ground black pepper
- 2 thick white bread slices, cubed
- 2 large heads romaine lettuce, torn
- 2 ripe avocados, pitted, peeled and sliced
- ½ cup Caesar dressing
- 2–3 tablespoons grated Parmesan cheese, for serving

1 Preheat air fryer to 380 F.
2 Brush chicken breasts with 2 tablespoons olive oil and season with plenty of salt and pepper.
3 Place chicken in air fryer basket and cook for about 20–25 minutes, turning once about halfway through, until chicken is golden brown and firm to the touch; it should register at least 165 F on a meat thermometer.
4 Remove chicken breasts from air fryer and let rest under foil for at least 5 minutes. Keep air fryer on.
5 Meanwhile, in a medium bowl, toss bread cubes with remaining 2 tablespoons olive oil and some salt and pepper to taste.
6 Arrange bread cubes in basket and cook until golden brown, about 6 to 8 minutes; shake basket once or twice during cooking.
7 Remove croutons from air fryer when done. Discard skin from chicken and cut meat into large chunks.
8 Divide romaine among 4 serving bowls and top with avocado, chicken chunks and croutons. Drizzle with dressing and sprinkle with grated Parmesan to serve.

GOURMET CHICKEN SANDWICH

COMFORT FOOD | CROWD-PLEASER

Toppings of bacon, feta and a bit of Caesar salad take this towering chicken sandwich to the next level.

Start to finish 30 minutes
(10 minutes active)
Servings 4

- 4 skinless chicken breasts
- ½ cup fine cornmeal
- 1 teaspoon smoked paprika
- Salt
- Freshly ground black pepper
- Cooking spray
- 4 smoked bacon slices
- 4 sesame seed burger buns, split
- 5 ounces (6 cups) mixed lettuces
- 4 tablespoons Caesar dressing
- ½ cup feta crumbles, or other soft cheese

1 Preheat air fryer to 380 F.
2 Place chicken breasts on a cutting board. Using a meat-tenderizer mallet, pound each breast to about ¼ inch thick.
3 In a shallow bowl, combine cornmeal, paprika and some salt and pepper to taste. Dust chicken with seasoned cornmeal, shaking off excess. Coat with cooking spray on both sides.
4 Place in basket and cook for about 20 minutes, turning after 10 minutes, until golden brown and cooked through; place bacon strips on chicken after about 14 minutes.
5 Remove from air fryer and keep chicken and bacon warm under foil.
6 Toast buns, if desired.
7 Meanwhile, in a large bowl, toss salad greens with Caesar dressing.
8 Arrange some salad on bottom halves of buns, placing chicken, bacon and some feta on top. Top with more salad and tops of buns before serving.

Chicken
Caesar Salad

SEE P.92

Hoisin and Honey
Glazed Salmon

FABULOUS

FISH & SEAFOOD

ENJOY THE BOUNTY OF THE SEA
WITH THESE MOUTHWATERING
DISHES THAT ARE FULL OF FLAVOR.

HOISIN AND HONEY GLAZED SALMON

CLASSIC | FAMILY FAVORITE

Sesame Broccoli and Cauliflower (page 117) makes a perfect side dish for this delightful entrée.

Start to finish 15 minutes (5 minutes active)
Servings 2

- 2 (8-ounce) salmon fillets, skin on
- ¼ teaspoon kosher salt
- ¼ teaspoon ground black pepper
- 1 tablespoon hoisin sauce
- 1 tablespoon honey
- 1 teaspoon soy sauce
- 1 teaspoon brown sugar
- 1 teaspoon minced garlic
- 1 teaspoon minced fresh ginger
- 1 teaspoon seasoned rice wine vinegar
  Cooking spray
- ½ teaspoon sesame seeds
- ½ teaspoon black sesame seeds
- ½ teaspoon chopped fresh cilantro
  GARNISH **Sliced scallions**

1 Preheat air fryer to 400 F.
2 Sprinkle fillets with salt and pepper.
3 In a small bowl, whisk together hoisin, honey, soy sauce, brown sugar, garlic, ginger and vinegar. Brush glaze all over each fillet.
4 Coat basket or rack of air fryer with cooking spray. Place fillets skin-side down in basket or rack.
5 Cook for 10 minutes. Remove and sprinkle with sesame seeds and cilantro; garnish and serve.

COD NUGGETS

CLASSIC | FAMILY FAVORITE

Cod is ideal for this recipe—it won't fall apart when cut into pieces and fried, and its mild, sweet flavor will tempt even the pickiest eaters.

Start to finish 30 minutes
(10 minutes active)
Servings 4

- ⅔ cup all-purpose flour
- 1 egg
- 1 cup dry breadcrumbs
  Salt
  Freshly ground black pepper
- 1 pound skinless cod fillet, cut into chunks
  Cooking spray
  Tartar sauce, for serving
  Potato wedges, for serving

1 Preheat air fryer to 380 F. Coat basket with cooking spray.
2 In a shallow bowl, add flour. In another bowl, beat egg. In a third bowl, add breadcrumbs. Season each with salt and pepper.
3 Dust cod chunks in flour, shaking off excess. Dip into beaten egg to coat, let excess drip off, and then dredge in breadcrumbs to coat.
4 Working in two batches, place half the nuggets in basket and coat with cooking spray.
5 Cook for 8 to 10 minutes until golden brown and crisp. Remove from air fryer and keep warm under foil.
6 When all nuggets are cooked, serve with tartar sauce and potato wedges on the side.

FRIED CALAMARI

EASY | PARTY FARE

This delicious appetizer will wow your guests and is ready in a jiffy.

Start to finish 20 minutes (2 minutes active)
Servings 4

- 1 (12-ounce) bag frozen breaded calamari
  Marinara or cocktail sauce, for serving
  GARNISH **Lemon slices**

1 Place calamari in air fryer basket or rack (you may need to work in batches).
2 Cook at 400 F for 8 minutes, shaking halfway through cooking time.
3 Place on serving plate; serve with marinara or cocktail sauce on the side and garnish with lemon.

A SQUEEZE OF LEMON ELEVATES THE FLAVOR OF SEAFOOD.

Fried Calamari

Blackened Tilapia
With Cucumber Salsa

Cook's Notes

Blackening seasoning is between Cajun (which is spicier) and Creole (which is made with more herbs) seasonings. It usually contains **paprika, cayenne, black pepper, sea salt, onion and garlic powders,** and dried herbs such as thyme, basil and oregano.

BLACKENED TILAPIA WITH CUCUMBER SALSA

CLASSIC | FAMILY FAVORITE

Red snapper or striped bass can be used instead of tilapia. Look for fillets that are similar in thickness for even cooking.

Start to finish 25 minutes
(10 minutes active)
Servings 4

> Cooking spray
4 (6-ounce) tilapia fillets
¼ cup blackening seasoning
1 tablespoon chopped cilantro
3 tablespoons chopped red onion
1½ tablespoons fresh lime juice
1 teaspoon extra-virgin olive oil
¼ teaspoon kosher salt
¼ teaspoon ground black pepper
1 cucumber, diced
GARNISHES Lime wedges, cilantro sprigs

1 Preheat air fryer to 400 F. Coat basket or tray with cooking spray.
2 Coat both sides of fillets with cooking spray; sprinkle blackening seasoning over both sides.
3 Arrange fillets in basket or tray (depending on shape of fillets, you may need to work in batches). Cook until fish flakes easily with a fork, about 6 minutes, depending on thickness.
4 In a medium bowl, combine cilantro, onion, lime juice, olive oil, salt and pepper. Let stand for 5 minutes, then add cucumber.
5 Top fish with salsa; garnish and serve.

SALMON WITH HORSERADISH CRUST

EASY | HEALTHY

The horseradish adds flavor and keeps the fish moist as it cooks.

Start to finish 25 minutes
(10 minutes active)
Servings 2

Fish Sticks

> Cooking spray
2 tablespoons prepared horseradish
1 tablespoon minced parsley
1 tablespoon capers, finely chopped
1 tablespoon extra-virgin olive oil
1 (12-16 ounce) skinless salmon fillet (about 1-inch thick)
½ teaspoon salt
¼ teaspoon ground black pepper

1 Coat air fryer basket or racks with cooking spray.
2 In a small bowl, stir together horseradish, parsley, capers and oil.
3 Sprinkle salmon with salt and pepper. Spread with horseradish mixture, then coat with cooking spray. Place in air fryer basket or rack.
4 Cook at 375 F for about 15 minutes, or until thickest part of salmon reads 130 F with a meat thermometer.
5 Let rest 5 minutes before serving.

FISH STICKS

EASY | KID-FRIENDLY

Old Bay is a classic seasoning blend designed for seafood. With a bit of spice and celery salt, it adds interest to this simple but delicious dish.

Start to finish 30 minutes
(15 minutes active)
Servings 4

> 4 (6-ounce) cod fillets
¼ cup flour
1 teaspoon paprika
1 teaspoon salt
½ teaspoon ground black pepper
2 eggs
1 cup panko breadcrumbs
1 tablespoon Old Bay seasoning
Cooking spray
Ketchup, tartar sauce, cocktail sauce, for serving

1 Cut each fillet into 4 sticks. Pat dry with paper towels.
2 In a shallow bowl, mix flour, paprika, salt and pepper. In another bowl, beat eggs. In a third bowl, mix breadcrumbs and Old Bay seasoning.
3 Coat fish sticks in flour mixture, then egg, then panko mixture, pressing to make panko adhere. Coat sticks with cooking spray.
4 Place sticks in air fryer basket or racks and cook at 400 F for 10 minutes, turning once halfway through.
5 Serve with ketchup, tartar sauce and/or cocktail sauce on the side.

CHECK OUT HOW GORGEOUS AND GOLDEN SALMON IS WHEN COOKED IN THE AIR FRYER!

Herbed Salmon Fillets

HERBED SALMON FILLETS

EASY | FAMILY FAVORITE

Heart-healthy salmon's rich flavor is enhanced by this slightly spicy herb topping. Look for wild-caught if it's available at your market.

Start to finish 15 minutes (5 minutes active)
Servings 2

- 2 (6-ounce) skinless salmon fillets
- ½ teaspoon salt
- ½ teaspoon ground black pepper
- 2 teaspoons olive oil
- 1 teaspoon paprika
- 1 teaspoon chili powder
- 1 teaspoon chopped parsley
- 1 teaspoon thyme leaves
  GARNISHES Thyme leaves, chopped parsley

1 Season salmon fillets with salt and pepper.
2 In a small bowl, whisk together oil, paprika, chili powder, parsley and thyme.
3 Spread on top of fillets.
4 Place fish in air fryer basket or rack.
5 Cook at 400 F for 10 minutes.
6 Garnish and serve.

CRABCAKES

CROWD-PLEASER | FAST FIX

Homemade crabcakes have a subtle sweetness and texture that can't be beat. Make them smaller if you're serving them as party appetizers.

Start to finish 25 minutes
(10 minutes active)
Servings 4

- 2 celery stalks, peeled and finely diced
- 1 scallion, finely chopped
- 2 egg whites
- 3 tablespoons mayonnaise
- ½ teaspoon salt
- ¼ teaspoon freshly ground black pepper
- 1¼ cups plain breadcrumbs, divided
- 12 ounces lump crabmeat, drained and picked through for shells

Cooking spray
Sour cream, for serving

- 1 tablespoon snipped chives, for serving
- 1 lemon, cut into slices or wedges

1 Preheat air fryer to 380 F.
2 In a mixing bowl, stir together celery, scallion, egg whites, mayonnaise, salt, pepper and ½ cup breadcrumbs. Gently fold in crabmeat. Divide mixture into 4 equal portions and shape each into a thick patty.
3 Place remaining ¾ cup breadcrumbs in a shallow dish; roll each patty in breadcrumbs, turning them to coat.
4 Coat basket with cooking spray. Working in batches if needed, arrange crabcakes in basket in a single layer. Coat with more cooking spray.
5 Cook for about 12 to 15 minutes, carefully turning after 7 to 8 minutes, until golden brown and crisp. Repeat cooking as needed for remaining crabcakes.
6 Serve with sour cream and chives on the side; garnish with lemons.

Crabcakes

SERVE CRABCAKES
AS A MAIN DISH, OR TRY
THEM IN SANDWICHES
WITH TARTAR SAUCE,
LETTUCE AND TOMATO.

97

Cook's Notes

Sour cream, dill and salmon are a perfect team, so why not try a sour cream and dill sauce? Just mix **chopped dill with sour cream**, add a little salt and freshly cracked black pepper, and a bit of lemon juice and zest.

SALMON CAKES

EASY | FAMILY FAVORITE

These salmon cakes look elegant when plated, but they're also perfect for sandwiches. Keep a can or two of salmon in the pantry and you can whip it up in no time.

Start to finish 25 minutes
(10 minutes active)
Servings 2

- 1 (14.75-ounce) can pink salmon, drained; bones and skin removed
- ½ cup panko breadcrumbs
- 2 tablespoons chopped dill
- 2 tablespoons mayonnaise
- 1 tablespoon Dijon mustard
- ½ teaspoon ground black pepper
- 1 egg
- Cooking spray
- Sour cream, for serving
- GARNISHES Lemon slices, dill sprigs

1 In a large bowl, add salmon, panko, dill, mayonnaise, mustard, pepper and egg. Stir gently to combine.
2 Shape mixture into two 6-inch patties. Coat patties with cooking spray.
3 Place in air fryer basket or racks and cook at 400 F for 10 to 12 minutes or until thermometer reads 160 F.
4 Place cakes on serving plates; top with sour cream, garnish and serve.

Bacon Wrapped Scallops

MAKE A BATCH OF THESE SCALLOPS FOR A PARTY APPETIZER.

BACON WRAPPED SCALLOPS

EASY | CLASSIC | PARTY FARE

These make an elegant meal alongside sauteed greens.

Start to finish 30 minutes
(15 minutes active)
Servings 4

- 8 slices center-cut bacon, halved
- 16 large sea scallops
  Cooking spray
- ½ teaspoon freshly ground black pepper

1 Preheat air fryer to 400 F.
2 Place bacon in air fryer basket or tray to partially cook for 3 minutes, flipping halfway through cooking. Remove from air fryer; set aside to cool.
3 Clean scallops; pat dry. Wrap each scallop in a half-strip of bacon; secure with toothpicks.
4 Coat scallops with cooking spray; season with black pepper.
5 Arrange scallops in a single layer in basket or tray (you may need to work in batches). Cook 8 minutes, flipping halfway through cooking, until scallops are opaque and bacon is crisp. Serve hot.

YOU'LL WANT TO DIP FRENCH FRIES AND HUSH PUPPIES IN THIS TARTAR SAUCE—SO MAKE EXTRA!

Southern-Style Catfish With Caper Tartar Sauce

SOUTHERN-STYLE CATFISH WITH CAPER TARTAR SAUCE

EASY | FAMILY FAVORITE

Serve this fish with classic sides, such as our Hush Puppies (page 120) or French Fries (page 123).

Start to finish 30 minutes
(10 minutes active)
Servings 4

- ¾ cup cornmeal
- 4 teaspoons Cajun seasoning, divided
- 4 (5-ounce) catfish fillets
- ½ cup mayonnaise
- ¼ cup capers
- 1 tablespoon lemon juice

GARNISHES **Lemon wedges, chopped curly parsley**

1 Preheat air fryer to 390 F.
2 In a gallon-size zip-close bag, combine cornmeal and 3 teaspoons Cajun seasoning.
3 Dry fillets with paper towels. Add to bag, 2 at a time, and shake to coat in cornmeal mixture. Repeat with remaining fillets.
4 Place fillets in air fryer basket or tray. Cook for 15 minutes, flipping halfway through.
5 Raise air fryer to 400 F; cook for 5 more minutes to brown fillets.
6 Meanwhile, in a small bowl, mix mayonnaise, capers, lemon juice and remaining Cajun seasoning to make tartar sauce.
7 Garnish and serve.

⌄ QUICK TIP

Fried catfish is an icon of Southern cuisine, especially when coated in cornmeal. But you can also coat the fish in panko or breadcrumbs.

LOBSTER TAILS WITH LEMON BUTTER

CLASSIC | FAMILY FAVORITE | PARTY FARE

Dinner guests will be impressed by these succulent lobster tails!

Start to finish 20 minutes (5 minutes active)
Servings 2

2	(4-ounce) lobster tails, butterflied
4	tablespoons butter
1	teaspoon lemon zest
2	cloves garlic, grated
1	teaspoon chopped parsley
	Lemon wedges, for serving

1 Preheat air fryer to 380 F.
2 Place lobster tails in basket or tray, meat-side up.
3 In a small saucepan over medium heat, melt butter. Stir in lemon zest and garlic; heat until garlic is tender, about 30 seconds.
4 Transfer 2 tablespoons of butter mixture to a small bowl and brush it onto lobster tails.
5 Cook 5 to 7 minutes or until lobster meat is opaque. Place on serving plates; spoon reserved butter over lobster meat.
6 Sprinkle with parsley; serve with lemon wedges.

FRIED CRAB BITES

KID-FRIENDLY | PARTY FARE

Serve a few of these mini crabcakes as a light main course with French Fries (page 123) and veggies, or delight your dinner guests by serving them as a fancy starter.

Start to finish 15 minutes (5 minutes active)
Servings 4

8	ounces jumbo lump crabmeat
⅓	cup panko breadcrumbs
¼	cup diced red bell pepper
1	egg
¼	cup mayonnaise
1	tablespoon lemon juice
1	tablespoon flour
1	tablespoon Old Bay seasoning
	Cooking spray
	Rémoulade, for serving
GARNISH	Lemon wedges

1 In a large bowl, mix crabmeat, breadcrumbs, pepper, egg, mayonnaise, lemon juice, flour and Old Bay seasoning.
2 Form into small balls. Coat with cooking spray.
3 Place in air fryer basket or racks and cook at 375 F for 10 minutes, turning once halfway through cooking.
4 Serve with rémoulade sauce and lemon wedges.

ROASTED SALMON FILLETS

FAMILY FAVORITE | FAST FIX

Cut cooking time by a few minutes if you prefer salmon more rare.

Start to finish 22 minutes
(10 minutes active)
Servings 4

1	large bunch scallions, trimmed
	Cooking spray
	Salt
	Freshly ground black pepper
4	skinless salmon fillets, pin-boned
2	tablespoons olive oil
1	handful fresh parsley, chopped
½	lemon, for serving

1 Preheat air fryer to 380 F. Coat scallions with cooking spray, turning to coat, and season with salt and pepper.
2 Arrange in basket and cook for 8 to 10 minutes until softened and starting to color, shaking basket a few times during cooking.
3 Remove from air fryer and keep warm under foil.
4 Season salmon fillets with salt and pepper and rub with olive oil. Place side by side in basket and cook for 10 to 12 minutes until firm to the touch and opaque in appearance.
5 Place a layer of scallions on a serving plate; top with salmon. Top with parsley and a squeeze of lemon juice to serve.

Roasted Salmon Fillets

SALMON FILLETS ARE ALSO DELICIOUS WITH DILL OR GARLIC BUTTER —OR TRY A TARRAGON BEURRE BLANC.

Fried Oysters
With Rémoulade

FRIED OYSTERS WITH RÉMOULADE

CLASSIC | COMFORT FOOD | FAMILY FAVORITE

If you're not comfortable shucking your own oysters, you can buy them pre-shucked.

Start to finish 25 minutes
(15 minutes active)
Servings 4

½	cup mayonnaise
½	cup sour cream
2	tablespoons Dijon mustard
1	tablespoon whole-grain mustard
1	tablespoon ketchup
1	teaspoon red wine vinegar
1	teaspoon hot sauce
2	teaspoons capers
1	scallion, thinly sliced
16	large oysters, shucked
2	cups flour
1	teaspoon salt
½	teaspoon ground black pepper
3	large eggs
2	tablespoons milk
1	cup cornmeal
	Cooking spray
	GARNISH Parsley leaves

1 Preheat air fryer to 400 F.
2 In a medium bowl, make rémoulade: Mix mayonnaise, sour cream, mustards, ketchup, vinegar, hot sauce, capers and scallion. Set aside.
3 In a shallow bowl, combine flour, salt and pepper. In a second bowl, beat eggs and milk. In a third bowl, add cornmeal.
4 Place several layers of paper towels on a baking sheet; set aside.
5 Pat oysters lightly with paper towels to dry. Dip each oyster into flour mixture to lightly coat, transfer to eggs and coat, then dip in cornmeal. Place on paper towel–lined baking sheet.
6 Transfer oysters to air fryer basket or tray (you may need to work in batches). Coat oysters with cooking spray and cook for 3 minutes. Flip and spray with cooking spray and cook an additional 3 minutes or until browned.
7 Serve warm with rémoulade; garnish with parsley leaves.

HAVE A TACO PARTY! SERVE ALL THE FIXINGS IN SEPARATE BOWLS SO YOUR GUESTS CAN BUILD THEIR OWN TACOS.

Fried Tilapia Tacos

FRIED TILAPIA TACOS

CROWD-PLEASER | PARTY FARE

Tilapia is low in saturated fat, high in protein and budget-friendly.

Start to finish 25 minutes
(15 minutes active)
Servings 4

	Cooking spray
1	pound skinless tilapia fillets, trimmed
½	cup cornstarch
2	teaspoons smoked paprika, divided
1	pinch red pepper flakes
1	egg
3	cups cornflakes, crushed
	Salt
	Freshly ground black pepper
4	tablespoons mayonnaise
1	lime, cut into wedges
4	6-inch flour tortillas
1	large avocado, pitted, peeled and sliced
1	red bell pepper, cored, seeded and cut into strips
1	cup red cabbage, shredded

1 Preheat air fryer to 400 F. Coat basket with cooking spray.
2 Thoroughly dry tilapia with paper towels. Cut into long strips.
3 In a shallow bowl, mix cornstarch, 1 teaspoon paprika and red pepper flakes. In a second bowl, beat egg. In a third bowl, add cornflakes. Season each with salt and pepper.
4 Dust tilapia with cornstarch mixture, shaking off excess. Dip in beaten egg, letting excess run off before dredging in cornflakes.
5 Place tilapia in basket in a single layer. Coat with more cooking spray.
6 Cook for 8 to 10 minutes until golden brown and crisp, carefully turning after 5 to 6 minutes.
7 Meanwhile, in a small bowl, stir together mayonnaise, a squeeze of lime juice, remaining 1 teaspoon smoked paprika, ½ teaspoon salt and 2 tablespoons warm water until smooth.
8 Remove tilapia from air fryer when ready and cover with foil to keep warm.
9 Briefly warm tortillas in air fryer. When ready to assemble, top tortillas with tilapia, avocado, pepper slices and cabbage.
10 Drizzle with spicy mayonnaise and serve with remaining lime wedges on the side.

⟩⟩ QUICK TIP

Use the air fryer to warm the tortillas, but be careful—they tend to burn easily at high temperatures.

SEARED SCALLOPS

FAST FIX | PARTY FARE

Get the largest sea scallops you can find for this dish. They are often more flavorful than smaller types and stay moist during cooking.

Start to finish 15 minutes
(10 minutes active)
Servings 4

- 8 sea scallops, roe removed
- 2 tablespoons canola oil, divided
- 1 teaspoon dried rosemary
  Salt
  Freshly ground black pepper
- 3 tablespoons extra-virgin olive oil
- 1 tablespoon balsamic vinegar
- 1 pinch sugar
- 1 tablespoon sesame seeds
  GARNISHES Orange segments,
  2 tablespoons fine lime zest

1 Preheat air fryer to 390 F.
2 Brush scallops with 1 tablespoon canola oil. Season with rosemary, salt and pepper.
3 Place in basket and cook for 2 minutes. Flip, brush with remaining canola oil, and cook for another 2 to 3 minutes until firm to the touch.
4 As scallops cook, in a small bowl, whisk together olive oil, vinegar, sugar and some salt to taste. Stir in sesame seeds to make dressing.
5 Arrange scallops on plates. Spoon dressing over top and garnish to serve.

CRAB CLAWS WITH AIOLI

EASY | FAMILY FAVORITE | PARTY FARE

You can find frozen crab claws in many big-box stores. Most of the shell is removed—except along one pincer, which makes a great handle for dipping these delectable treats.

Start to finish 25 minutes
(10 minutes active)
Servings 4

- ⅓ cup all-purpose flour
- 1 egg
- ½ cup panko breadcrumbs
- 24 cooked blue crab claws
  Cooking spray
- 3-4 cloves garlic
- 1 cup mayo
- 1 tablespoon lemon juice
  Salt
  GARNISH Sliced scallions

1 Preheat air fryer to 400 F.
2 In a shallow bowl, place flour. In a small bowl, beat egg. In another shallow bowl, place breadcrumbs.
3 Roll claws in flour. Dip each in egg, then roll in breadcrumbs.
4 Arrange coated claws in air fryer basket or tray (you may need to work in batches). Coat with cooking spray.
5 Cook for 13 to 15 minutes or until golden brown.
6 Make aioli: Finely mince garlic, then crush them into a paste. Mix with mayo; stir in lemon juice and salt.
7 Arrange on plates, garnish and serve.

SHRIMP FAJITAS

EASY | FAMILY FAVORITE | PARTY FARE

This dish comes together quickly, and if you serve the toppings on the side, everyone gets a custom meal.

Start to finish 30 minutes (10 minutes active)
Servings 4

- 1 red bell pepper, sliced into thin strips
- 1 green bell pepper, sliced into thin strips
- 1 red onion, sliced into thin strips
- 1 (1.12-ounce) package fajita seasoning mix, divided
- 4 tablespoons olive oil, divided
- 1 pound raw medium shrimp, peeled and deveined
- 4 (10-inch) flour tortillas, charred
  GARNISHES Sour cream, guacamole, salsa, cilantro

1 Preheat air fryer to 400 F.
2 In a large bowl, mix pepper and onion strips; sprinkle with half of fajita seasoning. Drizzle with 2 tablespoons olive oil; stir to combine.
3 In another large bowl, combine shrimp and remaining fajita seasoning. Drizzle with remaining olive oil; stir to combine.
4 Place vegetables in basket or rack of air fryer and cook for 12 minutes, shaking halfway through. Transfer mixture to a bowl and keep warm.
5 Place shrimp in basket or rack of air fryer and cook for 5 minutes. Flip and cook for additional 3 minutes.
6 Divide vegetables among tortillas; top with shrimp. Serve garnishes on the side.

FISH AND CHIPS WITH MALT VINEGAR

CLASSIC | EASY | FAMILY FAVORITE

The crunchy coating on the cod will have everyone digging in.

Start to finish 30 minutes
(10 minutes active)
Servings 2

- 1 pound cod, cut into 4 pieces
- ½ teaspoon kosher salt
- ½ teaspoon ground black pepper
- ½ cup all-purpose flour
- 1 egg
- 2 cups plain panko breadcrumbs
- 1 teaspoon seafood seasoning (such as Old Bay)
  GARNISHES Malt vinegar, lemon wedges, parsley leaves (optional)

1 Preheat air fryer to 400 F.
2 Pat fish dry with paper towels; season on both sides with salt and pepper.
3 In a shallow bowl, add flour. In a second bowl, beat egg. In a third bowl, mix breadcrumbs and seafood seasoning.
4 Coat fish in flour, then in egg, and finally in panko, pressing to adhere.
5 Place fish in basket or tray of air fryer and cook for 10 to 12 minutes, flipping halfway through, or until golden.
6 Serve with malt vinegar and French Fries (page 123). Garnish with lemon wedges and parsley leaves, if desired.

FOR A MORE SAVORY SIDE, OPT FOR TARTAR SAUCE INSTEAD OF MALT VINEGAR.

Fish and Chips
With Malt Vinegar

SUPER
VEGGIES
& SIDES

STUMPED FOR WHAT TO SERVE
WITH YOUR MAIN DISH, OR
LOOKING FOR NEW WAYS TO
PREPARE VEGGIES? WE'VE
GOT YOU COVERED.

SEE
P.110

Teriyaki Brussels
Sprouts

FRIED CAULIFLOWER

CROWD-PLEASER | PARTY FARE

Batter-dipped and fried, cauliflower is a savory snack or side dish; some aioli on the side makes it even better.

Start to finish 25 minutes
(10 minutes active)
Servings 4

¾   **cup all-purpose flour, plus extra for dusting**
1   **teaspoon garlic powder**
1   **teaspoon onion powder**
1   **pinch paprika**
½   **teaspoon salt**
¼   **teaspoon freshly ground black pepper**
½   **cup milk**
½   **cup water**
1   **cauliflower head, prepared into florets (see Quick Tip)**
    Cooking spray

1 Preheat air fryer to 390 F.
2 In a mixing bowl, stir together flour, garlic powder, onion powder, paprika, salt and pepper.
3 Gradually whisk in milk, then water, until batter is smooth and lump-free; whisk in more water if needed.
4 Dust florets with flour; shake off excess. Using a fork, drop into batter to coat.
5 Coat air fryer basket with cooking spray. Arrange cauliflower in basket in a single layer (you may need to work in batches).
6 Cook for 12 to 15 minutes until golden-brown and crisp, shaking basket a few times during cooking.
7 Remove from air fryer and let cool briefly before serving.

⌄
QUICK TIP

To easily prepare the cauliflower, cut off the stalk. Slice in half vertically, removing the core; the florets will separate on their own.

Spicy Green Beans

SPICY GREEN BEANS

CLASSIC | FAMILY FAVORITE | PARTY FARE

These Asian-inspired beans can be made without the red pepper flakes if you want to turn down the heat.

Start to finish 25 minutes
(10 minutes active)
Servings 4

- 1 **tablespoon sesame oil**
- 2 **teaspoons soy sauce**
- 1 **teaspoon seasoned
  rice wine vinegar**
- 1 **clove garlic, minced**
- ½ **teaspoon red pepper flakes**
- 1 **(12-ounce) bag trimmed
  green beans**
  GARNISH **Cilantro sprigs**

1 Preheat air fryer to 400 F.
2 In a medium bowl, whisk together sesame oil, soy sauce, vinegar, garlic and red pepper flakes. Add green beans and toss. Let marinate for 5 minutes.
3 Place green beans in air fryer basket (you may need to work in batches). Cook 12 minutes, shaking basket halfway through cooking time.
4 Place on serving dish; garnish and serve.

MEXICAN STREET CORN

CROWD-PLEASER | FAMILY FAVORITE

Kick up your corn on the cob! Mexican street corn is sweet, salty, cheesy and spicy—a perfect addition to your Taco Tuesdays.

Start to finish 25 minutes (5 minutes active)
Servings 4

- 4 **ears fresh corn on the cob, husks
  peeled back and silk removed
  Cooking spray**
- ½ **cup Cotija or feta cheese, crumbled**
- 1 **handful fresh cilantro, chopped
  Salt
  Freshly ground black pepper**
- 1 **pinch chili powder**
  GARNISH **Lime wedges**

1 Preheat air fryer to 390 F.
2 Coat corn with cooking spray, then place in air fryer basket.
3 Cook for 15 to 20 minutes, turning every 5 minutes, until corn is lightly charred.
4 Remove from air fryer and arrange on a serving platter. Top with cheese, cilantro, salt, pepper and chili powder. Garnish and serve.

QUICK TIP

If you prefer your corn neater, you can take the husks completely off—it makes removing the silk easier, as well.

Mexican
Street Corn

SESAME SEEDS ADD A BIT OF CRUNCH AND SOME HEART-HEALTHY FATS.

Sesame Broccoli
and Cauliflower

SESAME BROCCOLI AND CAULIFLOWER

CLASSIC | EASY | FAMILY FAVORITE

Chili-garlic sauce (sometimes called "rooster sauce" for the bird on the label) brings heat to these veggies.

Start to finish 20 minutes
(5 minutes active)
Servings 4

2	tablespoons vegetable oil
1	tablespoon sesame oil
1	tablespoon white miso
1	tablespoon chili-garlic sauce
1	tablespoon chopped parsley
2	teaspoons minced ginger
½	teaspoon kosher salt
1	cup broccoli florets
1	cup cauliflower florets
1	teaspoon sesame seeds
1	teaspoon black sesame seeds

1 Preheat air fryer to 400 F.
2 In a large bowl, stir together vegetable oil, sesame oil, miso, chili-garlic sauce, parsley, ginger and salt.
3 Add broccoli and cauliflower; toss well to coat.
4 Arrange vegetables in air fryer basket or tray. Cook for 15 minutes, gently tossing halfway through.
5 Transfer to a serving platter; sprinkle with sesame seeds and serve.

BROCCOLI WITH CHEESE SAUCE

COMFORT FOOD | EASY | FAMILY FAVORITE

Melted cheese makes broccoli even better!

Start to finish 15 minutes
(10 minutes active)
Servings 4

1	broccoli head, cut into florets
1	tablespoon olive oil
2	teaspoons kosher salt, divided
2	teaspoons freshly ground black pepper, divided
¼	cup butter
¼	cup flour
1½	cups heavy cream
1	tablespoon Worcestershire sauce
1	teaspoon paprika
1	teaspoon dry mustard
1½	cups grated cheddar cheese

1 Preheat air fryer to 325 F.
2 In a large bowl, toss broccoli, olive oil, 1 teaspoon salt and 1 teaspoon pepper.
3 Place broccoli in basket or tray of air fryer. Cook 4 to 5 minutes.
4 In a skillet over medium heat, melt butter; add flour and cook 2 minutes, stirring constantly. Add cream, Worcestershire sauce, paprika, dry mustard, and remaining salt and pepper.
5 Add cheese; stir until cheese melts and forms a smooth sauce.
6 Place broccoli in a serving bowl, pour in cheese sauce, toss and serve.

CRISPY ARTICHOKE HEARTS

EASY | PARTY FARE

These are delicious straight out of the air fryer, or dipped in horseradish aioli.

Start to finish 20 minutes
(10 minutes active)
Servings 4

1	(14-ounce) can artichoke hearts, drained and halved
1	tablespoon grated Parmesan cheese
1	teaspoon Italian seasoning
½	teaspoon kosher salt
¼	teaspoon ground black pepper
1	tablespoon olive oil
	Horseradish aioli

1 Preheat air fryer to 390 F.
2 In a large bowl, add artichoke hearts; sprinkle with Parmesan, Italian seasoning, salt and pepper. Drizzle with oil; toss to coat.
3 Place artichokes in air fryer basket or rack; cook for 4 minutes. Shake basket and continue cooking until artichokes begin to brown, 3 to 4 minutes more.
4 Serve with horseradish aioli.

MIX UP YOUR OWN SRIRACHA MAYO SO YOU CAN CONTROL THE SPICE LEVEL, OR BUY IT PREMIXED.

Beer-Battered Green Beans With Sriracha Mayo

Start to finish 20 minutes
(10 minutes active)
Servings 4

- 1 **pint shishito peppers (about 20), washed and patted dry**
- 1 **teaspoon olive oil**
- 1 **tablespoon soy sauce**
- 1 **tablespoon lime juice**
- 1 **teaspoon minced garlic**
- ½ **teaspoon minced ginger**
  GARNISH Chopped cilantro

1 In a large bowl, toss peppers with oil.
2 Place peppers in a single layer in air fryer basket or rack (you may need to work in batches).
3 Cook at 400 F, stirring halfway, until blistered and tender, about 7 minutes.
4 Meanwhile, in a small bowl, stir together soy sauce, lime juice, garlic and ginger. Add peppers and toss to coat.
5 Garnish and serve.

CREAMY MAC AND CHEESE

COMFORT FOOD | FAMILY FAVORITE

If you've never tried air fryer pasta, you'll be delighted to know that you don't have to cook it first when you make this creamy mac and cheese.

Start to finish 25 minutes
(5 minutes active)
Servings 4

- 1½ **cups dry elbow macaroni**
- 1 **cup water**
- ½ **cup heavy cream**
- 1 **(8-ounce) block cheddar cheese, shredded**
- 1 **teaspoon dry mustard**
- ½ **teaspoon salt**
- ½ **teaspoon ground black pepper**
  GARNISH Snipped chives

1 In a 7-inch round pan, stir all ingredients.
2 Place pan in air fryer basket or rack.
3 Cook at 360 F for 20 minutes, stirring halfway through.
4 Remove pan from air fryer. Let stand for 10 minutes, garnish and serve.

BEER-BATTERED GREEN BEANS WITH SRIRACHA MAYO

CROWD-PLEASER | PARTY FARE

A beer batter is lighter than other types, making it an ideal choice for delicate items such as green beans.

Start to finish 30 minutes
(10 minutes active)
Servings 4

- 1 **cup light beer**
- 1 **cup flour**
- 2 **teaspoons salt**
- 1 **teaspoon ground black pepper**
- 1 **(12-ounce) package fresh green beans, trimmed**
  Sriracha mayo (1 cup mayonnaise mixed with 3 tablespoons Sriracha)

1 In a medium bowl, mix beer, flour, salt and pepper. Add green beans; toss to coat. Shake off excess.
2 Place parchment in an air fryer basket or rack. Add beans to air fryer (you may need to work in batches).
3 Cook at 400 F for 10 minutes, turning once halfway through cooking.
4 Remove from air fryer. Serve with Sriracha mayo on the side for dipping.

GINGER SHISHITO PEPPERS

HEALTHY | PARTY FARE

You might think they'd be super spicy, but these small peppers are slightly sweet and generally mild in flavor. Make a few batches if you're serving them to a crowd —they go fast!

SPRINKLE ON SOME SNIPPED CHIVES FOR EXTRA COLOR AND FLAVOR. AND GO FOR TWISTY PASTA SHAPES LIKE THESE; ALL THOSE CURVES AND OPENINGS HOLD ON TO THE CHEESY GOODNESS!

Creamy Mac and Cheese

Cook's Notes

We served these hush puppies with a **spicy cocktail sauce**, but they'd also be tasty with a number of creamier options. Try them with a caper mayonnaise, an herbed aioli or a whole-grain mustard and honey sauce.

HUSH PUPPIES

CLASSIC | EASY | FAMILY FAVORITE

A mixture of cornmeal and flour helps hush puppies hold together, while maintaining their moist, fluffy center.

Start to finish 30 minutes
(10 minutes active)
Servings 12

	Cooking spray
1	**cup yellow cornmeal**
¾	**cup all-purpose flour**
1½	**teaspoons baking powder**
½	**teaspoon kosher salt**
¼	**teaspoon cayenne pepper**
¼	**teaspoon garlic powder**
2	**tablespoons minced onion**
¾	**cup buttermilk**
1	**egg**

1 Preheat air fryer to 390 F.
2 Line bottom of air fryer basket or rack with foil; coat with cooking spray.
3 In a large bowl, mix cornmeal, flour, baking powder, salt, cayenne, garlic powder and onion.
4 In a small bowl, whisk buttermilk and egg together. Stir into cornmeal mixture and let rest for 10 minutes.
5 Using a small cookie scoop, drop cornmeal mixture into basket or rack. Coat with cooking spray.
6 Cook for 10 minutes, or until browned. Place on a large plate to serve.

Veggie Tacos

Fried Green
Tomatoes

Cook's Notes

When making fried green tomatoes, always select the **firmest green tomatoes** (of any variety) you can find. Riper tomatoes give off lots of juice when you slice them, and they won't hold breading very well, especially when you fry them.

ROLL THE TOMATO SLICES
IN THE BREADCRUMB
MIXTURE TO GET PERFECTLY
GOLDEN EDGES LIKE THIS.

DELECTABLE

DESSERTS & SWEETS

WHO DOESN'T LOVE A TREAT
AT THE END OF A MEAL?
EVERYONE WILL LEAVE THE TABLE
HAPPY AFTER ENJOYING ONE
OF THESE GOODIES.

SEE
P.128

Chocolate-Glazed
Doughnuts

CHOCOLATE-GLAZED DOUGHNUTS

CLASSIC | EASY | KID-FRIENDLY

Bake the cutout centers to make doughnut holes, too!

Start to finish 20 minutes
(10 minutes active)
Servings 8

Cooking spray
1 (16.3-ounce) can refrigerated large flaky buttermilk biscuits
1 cup confectioners' sugar
2 tablespoons unsweetened dark baking cocoa
2 tablespoons melted butter
5 tablespoons milk
½ teaspoon vanilla extract
GARNISH **Sprinkles**

1 Preheat air fryer to 350 F. Coat basket or tray with cooking spray.
2 Separate biscuits and place on a cooking sheet. Use a 1-inch cutter to cut a hole in the center of each biscuit.
3 Place biscuit dough rounds in basket or tray (you may need to work in batches). Cook for 5 minutes. Cool on wire rack.
4 Meanwhile, in a small mixing bowl, combine confectioners' sugar, cocoa, melted butter, milk and vanilla to make glaze.
5 Dip cooled doughnuts in glaze, letting excess drip off. Place on wire rack; immediately top with sprinkles.

PEANUT BUTTER CUP BOMBS

CLASSIC | EASY | KID-FRIENDLY

Everyone loves this famous flavor combo!

Start to finish 18 minutes
(10 minutes active)
Servings 8

Cooking spray
1 (8-ounce) can refrigerated crescent rolls
8 (0.75-ounce) peanut butter cup candies
Confectioners' sugar

1 Preheat air fryer to 320 F. Coat basket or tray with cooking spray.
2 On a floured surface, unroll crescent dough. Place one peanut butter cup in the middle of each dough triangle.
3 Roll each into a ball, making sure candy is covered and seams are closed.
4 Place in basket or tray (you may need to work in batches). Cook for 5 to 8 minutes, or until browned.
5 Let cool slightly; dust with confectioners' sugar to serve.

SHORTBREAD STICKS WITH LEMON CURD

EASY | PARTY FARE

Lemon curd is intensely sweet and tart, making it a tasty dip for these shortbread sticks. They're also great dunked in coffee.

Start to finish 25 minutes
(15 minutes active)
Servings 4

1¼ cups flour
3 tablespoons sugar, plus additional to sprinkle
½ cup butter, chopped
Lemon curd, for serving

1 In a large bowl, stir together flour and sugar. Use a pastry blender to cut in butter until mixture is crumbly. Form mixture into a ball; knead until smooth.
2 Working on a floured surface, roll out dough to ¼ inch thick.
3 Cut dough into sticks about ½-inch wide and 3½ inches long. Sprinkle with additional sugar.
4 Arrange sticks in a single layer in air fryer basket or rack (you may need to work in batches).
5 Cook at 380 F for 3 to 4 minutes, or until lightly browned. Place on wire rack to cool.
6 Serve lemon curd on the side as a dip for the shortbread sticks.

TRY USING A MIX OF DARK AND MILK CHOCOLATE PB CUPS IN THESE BOMBS.

Peanut Butter Cup Bombs

Baked Apples

OPT FOR TART APPLE
VARIETIES,
SUCH AS WINESAPS
OR GRANNY SMITHS,
TO BALANCE THE
SWEET TOPPINGS.

Brownies

IF YOU PREFER YOUR BROWNIES TO BE MORE CAKE-LIKE THAN FUDGE-Y, ADD MORE FLOUR.

BAKED APPLES

FAST FIX | HEALTHY

Made with a touch of cinnamon and ginger, these apples have a bit of cream cheese in the center for an extra burst of flavor. Spoon some of the pan liquid over the top after you put each apple on a plate!

Start to finish 30 minutes
(10 minutes active)
Servings 4

- 4 Honeycrisp or Fuji apples
- ⅔ cup mixed dried fruit, such as raisins, sultanas and currants
- ½ cup whole almonds
- 2 tablespoons butter, melted
- 2 tablespoons honey
- 1 pinch ground cinnamon
- 1 pinch ground ginger
- 4 tablespoons cream cheese, softened

1 Preheat air fryer to 340 F.
2 Using a sharp paring knife held at a slight angle, remove cores from center of apples.
3 In a mixing bowl, toss together mixed dried fruit, almonds, butter, honey and spices.
4 Fill each apple with 1 tablespoon cream cheese and then evenly divide dried fruit and almond mixture on top.
5 Place in air fryer basket and cook for about 20 minutes until apples are tender to the tip of a knife.
6 Let cool briefly before serving.

BROWNIES

CLASSIC | KID-FRIENDLY

Who doesn't love these cakey, gooey chocolaty delights? Make them even more extra by topping each brownie with a big scoop of vanilla ice cream.

Start to finish 20 minutes
(5 minutes active)
Servings 4

- Cooking spray
- ½ cup flour
- 6 tablespoons cocoa powder
- ¾ cup sugar
- ¼ cup melted butter
- 2 eggs, beaten
- 1 tablespoon canola oil
- 1 tablespoon vanilla extract
- 1 teaspoon espresso powder
- ⅛ teaspoon salt
- ¼ teaspoon baking powder
- ½ cup semisweet chocolate chips

1 Coat a 6-inch-square cake pan with cooking spray.
2 In a large bowl, add flour, cocoa, sugar, butter, eggs, oil, vanilla, espresso powder, salt and baking powder. Stir until combined. Fold in chocolate chips.
3 Add batter to prepared pan.
4 Place in air fryer basket or rack. Cook at 325 F for 15 minutes or until a wooden pick inserted in the center comes out clean.
5 Let cool on wire rack before slicing and serving.

CRESCENT DOUGH SHEETS FROM THE REFRIGERATED SECTION OF YOUR GROCERY STORE MAKE THESE COOKIES A BREEZE!

Fried Oreos

2 tablespoons chopped pecans
1 tablespoon dark brown sugar
1 teaspoon flour
½ teaspoon cinnamon
GARNISH Vanilla ice cream or yogurt

1 In a bowl, toss pears and butter together to coat. Arrange wedges in a single layer in air fryer basket or rack.
2 In a small bowl, stir together pecans, sugar, flour and cinnamon. Sprinkle over pears.
3 Cook at 360 F for 12 minutes or until tender.
4 Top with ice cream or yogurt to serve.

CLASSIC S'MORES

CLASSIC | EASY | KID-FRIENDLY

No campfire handy? No worries with an air fryer! Eat these ASAP— they can get soggy if they sit.

Start to finish 10 minutes (2 minutes active)
Servings 4

4 whole graham crackers, broken in half
4 large marshmallows
2 (1.55-ounce) chocolate bars, broken in half

1 Place the 8 graham cracker halves in air fryer basket or rack.
2 Place a marshmallow on top of 4 of the crackers.
3 Cook at 390 F for 6 to 8 minutes or until marshmallow starts to crisp.
4 Remove from air fryer. Place a piece of chocolate on top of each marshmallow. Top with remaining graham crackers and press down. Serve immediately.

FRIED OREOS

CROWD-PLEASER | KID-FRIENDLY

Make this carnival treat at home— without the grease.

Start to finish 15 minutes (10 minutes active)
Servings 8

1 (8-ounce) can refrigerated crescent rolls
8 chocolate sandwich cookies
 Powdered sugar

1 On a cutting board, roll out dough, pressing down perforated lines to form one large sheet.
2 Cut the dough into 8 squares.
3 Place a cookie into the center of each dough square; fold up to cover all sides of cookie. Press down edges to seal.
4 Place cookies in air fryer basket or rack (you may need to work in batches) and cook at 320 F for 5 minutes or until golden.
5 Let cool on a wire rack, then sprinkle with powdered sugar to serve.

BROWN SUGAR ROASTED PEARS

HEALTHY | KID-FRIENDLY

Top these pears with ice cream for a special brunch treat.

Start to finish 20 minutes (5 minutes active)
Servings 2

2 pears, cored and cut in wedges
1 tablespoon butter, melted

QUICK TIP

Mix up your s'mores by using chocolate with almonds, toffee or peanut butter.

Classic S'Mores

WHEN BLUEBERRIES
ARE IN SEASON,
MIX FRESH ONES WITH
A SMALLER AMOUNT
OF PIE FILLING.

Cook's Notes

Not a fan of blueberries?
**You can sub in other fruit
fillings, such as cherry, peaches
or even chunky applesauce.**
For a healthier version, look
for fruit fillings that are made
with less sugar or have
no sugar added.

BLUEBERRY PIE
EGG ROLLS

FAMILY FAVORITE | PARTY FARE

**Pop these easy rolls into the air
fryer as you're finishing dinner
and they will be ready by the time
the coffee is fully brewed.**

Start to finish 20 minutes
(10 minutes active)
Servings 10

       Cooking spray
1   (16-ounce) package egg
       roll wrappers (20 per pack)
1   (21-ounce can) blueberry pie filling
       Confectioners' sugar

1 Preheat air fryer to 320 F. Coat
basket or tray with cooking spray.
2 On a cutting board, place 2 wrappers
so edges overlap (each egg roll uses
2 wrappers). Place 2 tablespoons of pie
filling in center of wrapper.
3 Dip a pastry brush in water; brush
all edges of wrappers with water, then
roll up, tucking sides in.
4 Repeat with remaining wrappers.
5 Place egg rolls in basket or tray,
leaving space between them (you may
need to work in batches). Cook for
5 minutes or until browned.
6 Dust with confectioners' sugar and
serve warm.

Cook's Notes

When you cut the centers out of the biscuits to make these doughnuts, **save the holes!** Cook them the same way as the doughnuts (for half the time), then glaze and coat them with sprinkles.

Glazed
Doughnuts

GLAZED DOUGHNUTS

EASY | KID-FRIENDLY

The glaze adds a bit of sweetness to these simple—but totally delicious—doughnuts. The dough isn't sweet, so it's a good contrast to the glaze.

Start to finish 14 minutes (2 minutes active)

Servings 8

- 1 (16.3-ounce) can refrigerated large biscuits
  Cooking spray
- 2 tablespoons milk
- ½ teaspoon vanilla extract
- 1 cup powdered sugar

1 Separate biscuits and place on a cooking sheet. Use a 1-inch cutter to cut a hole in the center of each biscuit.
2 Coat biscuits with cooking spray.
3 Place in air fryer basket or racks (you may need to work in batches) and cook at 350 F for 6 minutes, flipping halfway through cooking.
4 Meanwhile, in a shallow bowl, mix milk, vanilla and powdered sugar to make glaze.
5 Dip each doughnut in glaze and place on wax paper until glaze sets.

CARAMELIZED BANANAS WITH ICE CREAM

CLASSIC | EASY | FAMILY FAVORITE

The bananas keep their shape in the peels—and they make for an ap-peel-ing presentation, too!

Start to finish 10 minutes (2 minutes active)

Servings 2

- 2 bananas, peels on, sliced in half lengthwise
  Cooking spray
- 2 tablespoons dark brown sugar
  Ice cream (of your choosing)
  GARNISH Ground nutmeg

Cookies and Cream Cupcakes

1 Preheat air fryer to 350 F. Line basket or tray with parchment.
2 Coat banana halves with cooking spray. Sprinkle with brown sugar.
3 Place in basket or tray, cut-side up; cook for 6 minutes or until browned and caramelized.
4 Place 2 banana halves on each serving plate; top with ice cream and garnish to serve.

COOKIES AND CREAM CUPCAKES

EASY | KID-FRIENDLY

The ingredients in these cupcakes might surprise you, but the end result is amazing!

Start to finish 20 minutes (10 minutes active)

Servings 8

- 5 bananas, sliced
- 5 tablespoons cocoa powder
- 2 tablespoons sugar
- 4 eggs
- 1 small avocado, pitted and peeled
- 1 container cream cheese frosting
  GARNISH Crumbled chocolate sandwich cookies

1 Place bananas, cocoa, sugar, eggs and avocado in a blender and blend until smooth.
2 Pour batter into 8 greased silicone cupcake liners.
3 Place in air fryer basket or rack at 400 F for 7 minutes.
4 When completely cool, pipe frosting on cupcakes and sprinkle with cookie crumbles to serve.

QUICK TIP

If you want to make your cream cheese swirls look professional like these, treat yourself to a pastry bag and some piping tips.

STRAWBERRY-CHOCOLATE CAKE

EASY | FAMILY FAVORITE | KID-FRIENDLY

Add an extra spoonful of strawberry jam if you'd like!

Start to finish 25 minutes
(10 minutes active)
Servings 4

	Cooking spray
¼	cup sugar
4	tablespoons butter, softened
1	egg
1	tablespoon strawberry jam
6	tablespoons all-purpose flour
1	tablespoon unsweetened cocoa powder
⅛	teaspoon salt
	GARNISHES Chocolate sauce, sliced strawberries

1 Preheat air fryer to 320 F.
2 Coat a small, fluted tube pan with cooking spray.
3 In a large bowl, using an electric mixer, beat sugar and butter until light and creamy.
4 Add egg and jam; mix well.
5 Stir in flour, cocoa powder and salt; mix well. Pour batter into pan.
6 Place pan in basket or rack. Cook for 15 minutes or until a wooden toothpick comes out clean.
7 Let cool; drizzle with chocolate sauce. Garnish and serve.

CHERRY HAND PIES

COMFORT FOOD | EASY | KID-FRIENDLY

Sanding sugar's large crystals don't dissolve, giving these individual pies a sparkly finish.

Start to finish 26 minutes
(15 minutes active)
Servings 4

	Cooking spray
1	(16-ounce) package frozen puff pastry, thawed
½	cup cherry pie filling, divided
1	egg, beaten
	Sanding sugar, for sprinkling

1 Preheat air fryer to 350 F. Coat basket or rack with cooking spray.
2 On a floured cutting board, cut each pastry sheet in half.
3 Place 2 tablespoons pie filling in center of each sheet. Using a pastry brush, brush egg on all edges of sheet. Fold into triangles; using a fork, press to seal edges.
4 Coat with cooking spray; sprinkle with sanding sugar. Cook for 10 minutes or until pastry is browned.

BLUEBERRY PIE

CLASSIC | EASY | FAMILY FAVORITE

Be sure to defrost your pie crusts in advance so the pie bakes quickly.

Start to finish 30 minutes
(10 minutes active)
Servings 6

2	frozen pie crusts, thawed
2	(21-ounce) cans blueberry pie filling
½	teaspoon cinnamon
¼	teaspoon nutmeg
1	teaspoon milk

1 Check that crusts are pliable before using. Press 1 crust into a 6-inch pie tin.
2 In a large bowl, stir together pie filling, cinnamon and nutmeg. Pour into pie tin.
3 Cover with remaining crust, crimping edges to seal. Cut 4 slits in top of pie.
4 Brush top with milk.
5 Place in air fryer basket or rack and cook at 315 F for 15 to 17 minutes. Let cool slightly before serving.

⌄
QUICK TIP

Blueberries aren't just delicious; they're good for you, too. They're packed with lots of antioxidants. Eat up!

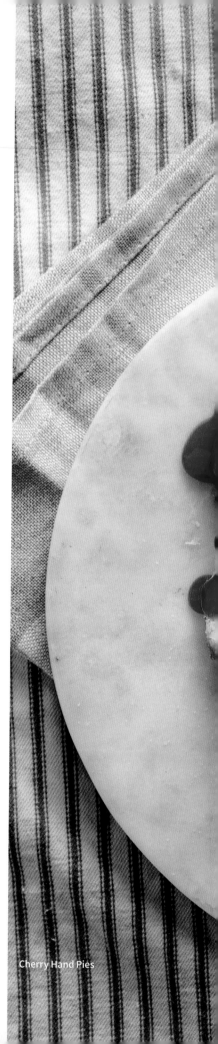
Cherry Hand Pies

THESE PIES ARE
BEST EATEN WARM, BUT
LET THEM COOL FOR
A FEW MINUTES BEFORE
SERVING BECAUSE
THE FILLING GETS HOT!

Cinnamon-Sugar
Doughnut Bites

CINNAMON-SUGAR
DOUGHNUT BITES

EASY | KID-FRIENDLY

**A few of these bites make a lovely
midafternoon snack with tea.**

Start to finish 10 minutes (5 minutes active)
Servings 20

    Cooking spray
1 (7.5-ounce) can refrigerated biscuits
½ cup sugar
2 tablespoons cinnamon

1 Coat the air fryer basket or rack with
cooking spray.
2 Unroll biscuits from can. Cut each
biscuit in half; roll into balls.
3 Place in air fryer (you may need
to work in batches). Cook at 350 F
for 2 to 3 minutes.

4 In a small bowl, mix sugar and
cinnamon. Roll bites in mixture
to serve.

PINEAPPLE WEDGES
WITH SLICED ALMONDS

EASY | FAMILY FAVORITE | KID-FRIENDLY

**In an air fryer, pineapple cooks up
tender and juicy. You can also use
canned chunks; drain the liquid first.**

Start to finish 27 minutes
(15 minutes active)
Servings 4

    Cooking spray
½ cup brown sugar
2 teaspoons cinnamon
1 pineapple, peeled, cored
    and cut into 8 spears

¼ cup melted butter
    Whipped cream, for serving
    Sliced almonds, for serving

1 Preheat air fryer to 400 F. Coat
basket or tray with cooking spray.
2 In a shallow bowl, mix brown sugar
and cinnamon.
3 Using a pastry brush, brush pineapple
with butter, then roll in cinnamon.
Press sugar to adhere. Place spears in
a single layer in bottom basket of air
fryer, leaving space between the spears
(you may need to work in batches).
4 Cook for 10 to 12 minutes or
until pineapple is heated through and
sugar is bubbling. Halfway through
cooking, brush pineapple with any
remaining butter.
5 Divide warm pineapple among
4 plates; top with whipped cream.
Pour remaining sauce over cream;
sprinkle with almonds and serve.

Cook's Notes

To cut a pineapple, use a sharp chef's knife. Cut off the top and base, then stand it on its base. **Use a smaller knife, such as a paring knife,** to cut off the spiky exterior. Now cut it in half, then quarters, vertically. Cut out the core on each quarter, then cut each quarter in half.

SLICED ALMONDS ADD A NICE CRUNCHY CONTRAST TO THE PINEAPPLE SLICES— PLUS, THEY'RE FULL OF GOOD FATS AND FIBER.

Pineapple Wedges
With Sliced Almonds

RECIPE INDEX

CREDITS

Photography William F. Dickey, II   **Styling** Margaret McLean

ADDITIONAL PHOTOGRAPHY

Waterbury Publications, Ken Carlson [Cover, 9]
Stockfood [Cover, 10–17, 31, 37, 39, 40–41, 44–47, 49, 52, 53, 56–57, 61, 88, 89, 97, 102–103, 105, 112–113, 122, 123, 130]

SEE
P.42

Mini Pepperoni
Pizzas

CENTENNIAL BOOKS

An Imprint of
Centennial Media, LLC
1111 Brickell Avenue, 10th Floor
Miami, FL 33131, U.S.A.

CENTENNIAL BOOKS is a trademark of Centennial Media, LLC

ISBN 978-1-951274-99-3

Distributed by
Simon & Schuster, Inc.
1230 Avenue of the Americas
New York, NY 10020, U.S.A.

For information about custom editions, special sales and premium and corporate purchases,
please contact Centennial Media at contact@centennialmedia.com.

Manufactured in China

10 9 8 7 6 5 4 3 2 1

Publishers & Co-Founders Ben Harris, Sebastian Raatz
Editorial Director Annabel Vered
Creative Director Jessica Power
Executive Editor Janet Giovanelli
Design Director Martin Elfers
Features Editor Alyssa Shaffer
Deputy Editors Ron Kelly, Amy Miller, Anne Marie O'Connor
Managing Editor Lisa Chambers
Senior Art Directors Lan Yin Bachelis, Pino Impastato
Art Directors Runyon Hall, Alberto Diaz, Jaclyn Loney, Natali Suasnavas, Joseph Ulatowski
Copy/Production Patty Carroll, Angela Taormina
Senior Photo Editor Jenny Veiga
Production Manager Paul Rodina
Production Assistants Tiana Schippa, Alyssa Swiderski
Editorial Assistants Michael Foster, Alexis Rotnicki
Sales & Marketing Jeremy Nurnberg